# CHILDHOOD REGAINED

D1607686

European Perspectives:
A Series of the Columbia University Press

# CHILDHOOD REGAINED

## The Art of the Storyteller

# FERNANDO SAVATER

TRANSLATED BY
Frances M. López-Morillas

1982
COLUMBIA UNIVERSITY PRESS
NEW YORK

Published with the assistance of the
Comité Conjunto Hispano-Norteamericano
para Asuntos Educativos y Culturales


The following illustrations are reprinted by permission:

Page 92: "War of the Worlds" cover illustration by Frank R. Paul, *Amazing Stories* (August 1927) Vol. 2, No. 4, reprinted with permission of Ultimate Publishing Co., Inc.

Page 114: Reprinted with permission of Macmillan Publishing Co., Inc., from *The Star Rover*, by Jack London, illustrated by Leonard Everett Fisher. Copyright © 1963 Macmillan Publishing Co., Inc.

Page 124: "The Elven King's Gate," reprinted with permission of Houghton Mifflin Co. and George Allen & Unwin, Ltd., from *The Hobbit*, by J. R. R. Tolkien. Copyright © 1966 J. R. R. Tolkien.

Library of Congress Cataloging in Publication Data
Savater, Fernando.
Childhood regained.

(European perspectives)
Translation of: La infancia recuperada.
Includes bibliographical references.
1. Fiction—History and criticism.
I. Title. II. Series.
PN3491.S2813     1981     809.3     81-12218
ISBN 0-231-05320-7          AACR2


Columbia University Press
New York     Guildford, Surrey
Copyright © 1982 Columbia University Press
*La infancia recuperada,* Taurus Ediciones, S. A., 1976, 1977, 1979
Copyright © 1979 Fernando Savater

To my son Amador Julián,
for whom I am the sentinel of tales

# CONTENTS

La littérature . . . c'est enfance enfin retrouvée.

Georges Bataille, La Littérature et le mal.

The King opened the book. . . . "O physician, there is no writing here!" Duban replied, "Turn over yet more"; and he turned over three others in the same way. Now the book was poisoned; and before long the venom penetrated his system, and he fell into strong convulsions, and he cried out, "The poison hath done its work!" Whereupon the Sage Duban's head began to improvise:

> There be rulers who have ruled with a foul, tyrannic sway
> But they soon became as though they had never, never been:
> Just, they had won justice: they oppressed and were opprest
> By Fortune, who requited them with ban and bane and teen:
> So they faded like the morn, and the tongue of things repeats,
> Take this for that, nor vent upon Fortune's ways thy spleen.

No sooner had the head ceased speaking than the King rolled over dead.

The Thousand and One Nights, Burton Trans.

# PROLOGUE

THIS IS a deliberately subjective book; that is, a book in which subjectivity has been used as a method, not only as an irreducible residue or mere ornament. What I am trying to do here, therefore, is certainly not to perform scientific research on literary texts—the sort of research that arouses such enthusiasm in those who are fascinated by the spectacularly useless. Ignorance protects me—though not as much as I would like—against linguistics, semiotics, stylistics, computer science, and sociometrics. There are no diagrams here: those who know no geometry are welcome. Whoever is chiefly interested in the signifier and the signified, in literalness, in enunciation, in prosopography, and in connotative axes has reached his Deadly Desert; let him retreat while he still has strength to get to the nearest generative grammar. What this book most closely resembles is a volume of memoirs, and in a certain sense that I will spell out later, it is about memory, narrative memory. It is, then, a book of memories, not a scientific treatise but a souvenir book.

The reader who has not yet thrown down these pages in irritation, probably out of inertia or the miserly desire to recover in some way the sum that he has foolishly invested in their purchase, will now receive a new and justifiable chance to avoid so superfluous a piece of reading. Let him consult the biobibliographical appendix at the end of the book; if the authors listed there are not his special favorites or if he does not even recognize their names, if the archetypal images of his mythical stage set are not centered on them and he thinks of them as modest manufacturers of harmless little tales for children, then this book is of absolutely no interest for him. He must not be deceived into taking this statement as circumstantial speech-making by the author and can stop reading with a clear conscience, using these lines as a certificate of literary good conduct if he wishes.

Among the survivors of these successive screenings I seem to perceive the presence of a deluded enthusiast who would do well to step down at once. This fellow concedes that the authors dealt with herein can have interest as *symptoms* and that they permit readings somewhat more profound than the ones usually assigned to them by entranced adolescents. He belongs to the class of degenerates who go to see Buster Keaton movies because they contain penetrating satires on the American Mom or who started to read comics at the age of thirty in order to flesh out their study on the repressive function of the mass media. Their standard-bearer is an imbecile who on a certain occasion, when he heard that I was writing about Stevenson, commented approvingly, "Fine, because *Treasure Island* is only a pretext." Let me make it clear, therefore, that I like these storytellers for the same reasons that children do; that is, because they tell wonderful yarns and tell them well, that I know no loftier reason than this to read a book, and that in literature I avoid sociologies and psychoanalysis as much as possible, so that my liver will not take umbrage.

Advocates of demythification should also abstain. In this book nothing is demythologized except the compulsive need to demythologize, the passion of persons who do not know what a myth is—Justice and Equality are myths, neither more nor less gloriously and inescapably than Honor, Nobility, and Courage—and who haven't the talent for free creation, which is what is most thoroughly reviled nowadays. Demythification has become a technique for cutting literature down to size; it is absolutely compatible with the dominant mythical image of rationalist and progressive society. This has little to do with criticism of the false places where myth is made to appear or with protest over its reduction to consoling or apologetic uses of Death; for this task, which is simultaneously critical and

creative, can be undertaken from the viewpoint of full acceptance of the mythical confrontation with Death itself.

Now that the scientists, the symptomologists, and the de-
mythologizers are out of the picture, I think that we are among
friends. Now I need only clarify what I want to do in this book,
since I seem to have rejected the most sacred viewpoints of the
criticism and laying-bare of texts. Very simply, the only thing
I want to do is provoke an evocation, a sort of literary spell.
What is evoked is not merely the written reverberation of the
great stories but in particular the state of mind which seeks
them out and revels in them, along with the joyous imprint left
on the memory by reading them. To accomplish this evocation
I have purposely used subjectivity as my point of departure,
as I said before, utilizing everything that tickles it, alarms it,
or is recognizable by it: I use quotations (preferring the version
offered by my memory rather than the one corroborated after
consulting the text) but also more or less obvious pastiches,
personal anecdotes indissolubly connected with the first flush
of reading a certain story, and admittedly arbitrary paraphrases
of some memorable episodes. The illustrations that accompany
the text are also meant to accomplish the same purpose. I am
attempting by these means to reconstruct—evoke—the story's
ethical level, its fundamental importance in the acquisition of
a moral sense which is not aimed first and foremost at a timid
correction of customs but leads to what is meant by the Spanish
expression *tener la moral alta, tener mucha moral* [to have high
morale, lots of morale]: rebellion in the face of blind necessity,
in the face of the crushing weight of inhuman circumstances
which seem to leave no room for the human factor, the free
courage that confronts routines and mechanisms alien to itself
and succeeds in affirming the predominance of the marvelous,
of the immortal. This is the attitude of Joseph Conrad's sailor,
who manages to keep control of himself during a typhoon and
achieves a sense of vigilant security: "The distant muttering of
the darkness stole into his ears. He noted it unmoved, out of
that sudden belief in himself, as a man safe in a shirt of mail
would watch a point."

I have followed no easily describable criterion for the selection of the characters I have evoked. All the characters in the book are ones I like, but I have left out many others who are equal favorites. What excuse have I for omitting Dick Turpin, Ivanhoe, or the Three Musketeers? Rudyard Kipling and James Oliver Curwood are mentioned only in passing and do not have a chapter to themselves. I attempt to justify the exclusion of Tarzan, a character who is undoubtedly one of the closest to my heart, by the existence of a complete study written by Francis Lacassin; I am aware of the feebleness of this excuse. I know that the ultimate reason for these omissions is laziness; I would like to think that I have also been influenced by a certain vague fear of repetition and the memory of Voltaire's warning, "the secret of being boring is to tell all."

On the other hand, the inclusion of a few pages on Jorge Luis Borges may be surprising, for his admirable tales are too self-conscious to be considered "stories" in the sense given to the word in this book. However, Borges has thought through the narrative function as few other writers have done. He is without question one of the shrewdest and most sensitive readers who have ever existed. In the always relevant humor of his commentaries, I have learned to recall and evaluate what I have read, and so this book owes its very existence to him. This volume would be far from complete if it left out the man who wrote, "All literature is symbolic; there are a few fundamental experiences, and it does not matter whether, in order to transmit them, a writer resorts to 'the fantastic' or to 'the real,' to Macbeth or Raskolnikov, to the invasion of Belgium in 1914 or to an invasion from Mars."

I fear that at times nostalgia for the pristine wonderment with which I read for the first time the tales here evoked has made me fall into the sin of excessive affirmation, of facile enthusiasm. It was inevitable: like Merleau-Ponty, I too will never be able to recover from my incomparable childhood. At any rate, no matter how theoretically dangerous this may be eventually, I want to stay faithful to what I have enjoyed. Many friends have encouraged me to write this book, which will inevitably disappoint them; they love the seductive power of these tales so

much that they will never be content with this pallid and la-
borious evocation of them. And so I want to beg their pardon
as Ezra Pound did at the end of his *Cantos*, for having tried to
recreate Paradise: "Let those I love try to forgive / what I have
made."

San Sebastián, August 1976

# I

# THE STORYTELLER ESCAPES

I F I KNEW HOW TO TELL you a good story, I would tell it. Since I don't know how, I am going to tell you about the best stories that have been told to me. The teller of stories has always just arrived from a long journey during which he has experienced both marvels and terrors. Just as the innocent Enkidu saw his sylvan existence troubled by a hunter whom he met near the watering place and who was the first human being he had met in his life. The poem says that "grief made way into his heart, / And he looked like a wanderer of far ways."[1] Thus, behind the visage of the wanderer of far ways waits the dark flow of stories. But the journey has not always allowed the traveler to be the adventure's protagonist; often he has had to content himself with hearing the tale from another's lips, the two of them seated before a jug of beer in the tavern full of people and smoke, or with listening to the convulsive whispers that issue from the lips of a dying man whose eyes have begun to be acquainted with ghosts. Maybe he has read the astounding story in the manuscript found in a bottle, or in that accursed book of spells which the bookseller has very sensibly refused to sell. I cannot boast of anything of the sort. I read the stories I am going to tell you about in books I acquired very simply, by purchase or theft, in perfectly ordinary establishments.

No, that isn't true; nothing was so prodigious as that little shop in Calle de Fuenterrabía, in San Sebastián, that was the navel of the world when I was seven or eight years old. Thomas de Quincey claims that the apothecary who sold him his first grains of opium was a shining angel beneath his ordinary, sleepy appearance. Must I not think the same of the person who one day placed in my hands a little volume bound in red leather—disturbing ambiguity—that contained the adventures of Sherlock Holmes? At the back of the shop, behind the counter, was the complete collection of Emilio Salgari's works, with Oriental maps inside the covers. Sometimes, in summer, a little old man with a white goatee would come in and buy detective stories he called his "sleeping pills"; the woman who owned the shop would tell me in a whisper of veneration, "That is Don Jacinto Benavente!" And I, who naturally had neither read nor seen any play by Don Jacinto (neither then nor now, if the truth be told), felt a shiver of admiration because I have always been easily inclined to the veneration of great men and, for fear that there might not be any or that the few who are left may run out, I am ready to concede that title even to those who may not deserve it more than anybody else. In that bookshop I bought *A Journey to the Center of the Earth* in a modern edition, very ugly and without illustrations, but which I cannot see to this day without feeling my throat tighten with danger and emotion. And also the first novels I read of James Oliver Curwood (*The Grizzly King, Kazan, The Courage of Captain Plum*) and Zane Grey. Don't worry, I'm not going to recount my memoirs. I only want to tell you, so that you'll listen to me more sympathetically, that to a very modest degree I too have come from far ways, just as all men can say in some sense, owing to time and its vicissitudes. What I am beginning here is the record of a journey; after all, I want to think that I too am going to tell you a story.

For the problem is that not everyone who begins to tell us something really has a story to tell. When I discovered this simple truth I was completely taken aback. Years later I relived that stupefaction in my little brother, who one day picked up a philosophical essay that I had on my study table and asked, "Does this have a plot?" to which I replied, with unpardonable levity, that it did not, and he answered, "Then I can't imagine how it can be a book." He was right, of course, and overcoming this initial astonishment is the first difficulty in the path of anyone who wants to read philosophy.

However, if the philosopher really tells something—that is, if he is any good—what he tells is a story. In the last resort it is much easier to ascribe a philosophical system to the narrative genre than many novels. *Phenomenology of Spirit*, for example, is a story by definition, but so are Vico's *New Science*, Leibniz' *Theodicy*, and of course Spinoza's *Ethics*. What varies is the way of telling it. Philosophy's narrative status resolves the positivist doubt which asks of each speculative development, "And who is telling me this?" to which the philosopher-storyteller replies, "I am saying it"; but he formulates this reply in a more exact form—"Listen not to me but to the *logos*,"—which might well become the narrator's motto.

But that early astonishment to which I referred, the one that discovered the absence of a story, was not brought home to me by philosophical texts—I never read an essay until I was seventeen or eighteen—but by novels, those "serious" novels which my mother read and which I occasionally leafed through behind her back. I remember that when I was twelve or thirteen years old I had a private tutor in Latin, a young man who was studying law, with whom I carried on great talks about every-thing under the sun. I thought that the things he said were the last word on every subject, because he had revealed the strange secret of sex to me. Literature was one of our most recurrent subjects; one day I told him that my favorite novel—what I said was "the best book I ever read"—was *Moby-Dick* and asked him what his favorite book was. He spoke enthusiastically of Gironella's *The Cypresses Believe in God*, which had just been published. I thought it was perfectly ridiculous to compare that boring blockbuster of a novel, with its stupid title and irrelevant plot, to the epic of the *Pequod*, but he, with a benevolent smile for my scant years, told me that when I grew up I would think differently. I cannot remember ever having been as sure of anything as I was then, that the passage of time would never make me place Gironella above Melville, and on that day my mentor's star began to decline in my esteem.

I can state with satisfaction that I still have not changed that opinion of mine, though I now know a good deal more about the kind of literature my teacher preferred. If I had had to explain my judgment at that time I would have said something like this: that nothing happened in Gironella's book, it told nothing interesting, compared with the extraordinary story of Ahab and his whale. But this opinion is not easy to uphold, especially if we substitute for *The Cypresses Believe in God* a work of greater literary merit, such as, for example, Proust's *Remembrance of Things Past*. Gironella too—or Proust—tells something, and even something that is more useful, something on a higher and more serious plane than the hunt for a whale. Perhaps it simply means that I described—and still describe—a story that I do not understand as the lack of a story. This probably requires a more careful analysis.

To make a first stab at the subject, I call "story" those themes which interest children: the sea; the accidents of the chase; the responses of cunning or energy called up by danger, physical intrepidity, loyalty to friends or to obligations incurred; protection of the weak; a curiosity that is willing to risk life to find satisfaction; a taste for the marvelous and the fascination of the terrible; a sense of brotherhood with animals; and so on. I suppose that this is residual romanticism, or, as a sociologist would say in his arrogant jargon, an exaltation of the individualistic and rapacious virtues of the feudal period, recreated for the purposes of petit-bourgeois escapism. Naturally there must be some truth in this, if the experts say so. No doubt there is an unsuccessful attempt to recover the realm of the preconventional or, if you prefer, the primary conventions, in contrast to that world of "secondary conventions," around which storyless novels turn. To continue with the obligatory sociology, I mean those conventions which arise from establishment of the bourgeoisie's ascendancy and have their best plot manifestations in Flaubert's or Stendhal's novels: adultery, economic prosperity, adaptation or lack of adaptation to the social milieu, religious problems, the triumph of honorableness and hard work or the defeat of both by injustice, psychological confusions of every stripe, the marks left by poverty or vicious corruption, and so on.[2] The same set of problems has persisted into our century, with an accentuation if you like of political confrontations and sexual experimentation. "Stories," in the sense I mentioned above, have been downgraded into subliterature, considered as suitable only for consumption by dreamy adolescents and an adult audience with few pretensions to culture.

Naturally I am not trying to feign lack of interest or scorn for that kind of storyless literature consecrated by the taste of our times, and hence I have hastened to substitute Flaubert or Proust for Gironella so that there can be no doubt about the esteem that the most widely cultivated genre of the past two hundred years deserves—from me as from anyone else. But, and this is my "small difference," I continue to be unswervingly faithful to the narrative world of my childhood, to the stories that established the primary objects of my subjectivity. I do not believe that my sensitivity in this respect is in any way unique. As proof, let us look at a speech Michael Innes places in the mouth of one character in his excellent detective story *Hamlet, Revenge!*:

I see the difference in my own waking and dream life. My waking life is given to imaginative writing—writing in which the chief concern is values. But my dreams, like melodrama, are very little concerned with values. The whole interest is on a tooth and claw level. Attack and escape, hunting, trapping, outwitting. A consciousness all the time of physical action, of material masses and dispositions as elements in a duel. And, of course, the constant sense of obscurity or mystery that haunts dreams.[3]

I think that Innes understands here by values what I have just called "secondary conventions," for, as we shall soon see, pure stories do not ignore a certain kind of values, indeed quite the opposite. I find the allusion to the world of dreams especially relevant in characterizing the fundamental stories with which I am dealing here. In a sense, stories break down the conventional wall of everydayness and spread before the reader, as H. P. Lovecraft said in one of his sonnets, "all the wild worlds of which my dreams had told."

To rise above this elementary level of presenting the question, I will climb onto the shoulders of one of our time's keenest readers, Walter Benjamin. Benjamin has a simply splendid short essay on the themes that I have laboriously tried to sketch here. I shall permit myself the luxury of paraphrasing it at some length, for its penetration will aid my clumsy efforts and spare us many a misguided groping and unnecessary digression. The short essay in question bears the title of "The Storyteller."[4] Benjamin understands by "storytelling" more or less what I have called "story" here, in contrast to the bourgeois genre of the novel. At the beginning of his study he gives this superb description: "And among those who have written down the tales, it is the great ones whose written version differs least from the speech of the many nameless storytellers." This emphasizes the essential relationship between narration and memory or, better still, between the forms consolidated in memory as opposed to the novel, which is in large measure invention or, what comes to the same thing, innovation. The storyteller is talking about something that he has no right to change substantially at his own discretion; the only right that the novelist has to talk of what he talks about is fidelity to the changes which his discretion places on what is being told. The storyteller transmits but does not invent. What does he transmit? The experience that is passed by word of mouth, says Benjamin; and I would say that it transmits men's hope in their own possibilities.

As has been said, there is no hope if not in memory: there lie the victories and the lessons of defeat, the overcoming of what seemed impossible, the favorable or unfavorable intervention of the gods, the annihilation of all tyrants, the resources of cunning and courage. The storyteller must keep alive the most improbable flame, that of hope, and hence he cannot alter according to his own whim the message that others have handed down to him. Hope cannot be played with, though only hope permits free play. No task is more alien to the storyteller than demythification, which is precisely the modern novelist's primary task—the task even of those who, nowadays, are engaged in demythologizing demythification, so that instead of getting closer to ordinary narration, they can superimpose new stages that take them further and further away from it. Therefore, because it is both hopeful and hope-imparting, storytelling is incurably ingenuous. But its ingenuousness is fundamentally etymological: it comes from that Latin *ingenuus* whose etymological meaning is "noble, generous" and, specifically, "freeborn," as stories are freely born and freely transmitted in the noble and generous task of storytelling.

Later in his essay Benjamin writes, "An orientation toward practical interests is characteristic of many born storytellers." And, a little further on, "All this points to the nature of every real story. It contains, openly or covertly, something useful. The usefulness may, in one case, consist in a moral; in another, some practical advice; in a third, a proverb or maxim. In every case the storyteller is a man who has counsel for his readers." Practical interest and wise counsel form part of the essentially hopeful nature of storytelling. The storyteller includes his hearer in the story itself, as a future protagonist, and warns him of dangers which by the mere fact of listening he has already begun to experience. The best part of an adventure tale is to sense it as a prologue and initiation of our own adventure. Hence the interest in practical details, whose usefulness may become essential for us.

To emphasize this preparatory nature of storytelling, many stories begin with a tale that places the protagonists on the road and offers them advice that will save them from future dangers: the sinister saga told by old Bill to Jim Hawkins, recounting the vicissitudes of Flint's treasure and warning him against the seafaring man with one leg; or the dying man's story that starts off the amazing adventure of *King Solomon's Mines*, written "in a plain, straightforward manner" by Allan Quatermain; or the map and markings on the rocks which the long-dead Arne Saknussemm leaves behind him to encourage and guide the travelers to the center of the earth. Storytellers tell their story as if their hearers were about to start off on a journey. This is the reason for the scientific descriptions of Jules Verne or Emilio Salgari, who recommend the medicinal properties of this or that fruit or warn against the menace of this or that tribe of cannibals, as if the reader were going to run risks identical to those of the protagonist of their stories the day after reading them. Some of Salgari's tales resemble a *Guide Bleu* for the use of adventurers in Hindustan or the Matto Grosso.

Naturally, the ability to offer counsel depends on the validity of the storyteller's own experience or of his perfect fidelity to the memory that preserves what he is transmitting. If no one has any faith in his experiences, and weary skepticism undermines the foundations of memory, his advice becomes a mockery or opens the door to despair. In just such a way, the accumulated experience of all his reading betrays Don Quixote, for not only does it fail to help him out of any difficulty but contributes toward defeating him. The modern novel was born to tell of the discomfort experienced by the man who has been betrayed by all stories, by memory itself. What is degraded is the truth itself, and hence no advice is true. "Counsel woven into the fabric of real life is wisdom. The art of storytelling is reaching its end because the epic side of truth, wisdom, is dying out." The other side of truth is science, which no longer advises but legislates, and which has wiped out the strong ethical stamp retained by experience lived through the lesson of the story. From wisdom that has been won we progress to information that has been acquired.

Among the different traits which mark the difference between storytelling and novel, says Benjamin, "What distinguishes the novel from the story (and from the epic in the narrower sense) is its essential dependence on the book." Storytelling still preserves the presence of the man who advances toward the firelight and the avid circle of his hearers. This is more than a metaphor: it alludes to the fact that a story can always be read aloud, indeed there is no other way to read it. In the novel, the book is a hiding place and the scene of a withdrawal; a solitude has sought to nestle in the inviolable silence of its pages. The contents of a novel cannot really be told by voice, while all stories, even when read alone, are really being told in living words. Let me point out that in this respect philosophy also lies down at the side of storytelling, for it too belongs to the epic side of truth. The contrasting relationship which novel and story possess with regard to the book is rooted in the very origin of both: "The storyteller takes what he tells from experience—his own or that reported by others. And he in turn makes it the experience of those who are listening to his tale. The novelist has isolated himself. The birthplace of the novel is the solitary individual, who is no longer able to express himself by giving examples of his most important concerns, is himself uncounseled, and cannot counsel others." Storytelling demands a community in order to exist, though it may be the sudden and unexpected one created, by pity on the one hand and misfortune on the other, between the shipwrecked man and the person who rescues him on the beach; the novelist, on the other hand, is apt to intone a lament for lost community. It is possible for storytelling's theme to be solitude, but from the very point when solitude begins to be recounted it is wiped out, not only in the fleeting moment of the tale's duration but in the future that promises the possibility itself of storytelling.

In its present solitude the novel maintains the narrative habit it once denied, like the philosopher of the cynic school who continued to talk imperturbably after his chance interlocutor had gone away and left him.

On the other hand, storytelling must also be clearly distinguished from informative exposition, which it may approach in its taste for practical detail. In our time the primacy of information has contributed decisively to the fact that the art of storytelling has become rare. In the first place, it imposes an abstract verisimilitude, of immediate verification, which has nothing to do with narrative plausibility: "But while the latter [storytelling] was inclined to borrow from the miraculous, it is indispensable for information to sound plausible. Because of this it proves incompatible with the spirit of storytelling." A story's aim always includes a more or less generous broadening of the circle of customary expectations, while information tends first of all to confirm that our concept of the possible is adequate. At least in the remote country or for the righteous man, for the powerful magician or the friend of the gods, necessity suspends its laws in storytelling, thus opening up a fissure in the need for the necessary: information resigns itself in advance to observance of necessary laws. Hence storytelling establishes its own law as the highest law in every case, while information is the voice itself of law confirming itself in every instance.

Since the essence of that which information transmits is always identical, the necessity of law, pure incidental novelty, is the substance that in each case is intended for transmission, and beyond that nothing remains but the law itself. "The value of information does not survive the moment in which it was new. It lives only at that moment; it has to surrender to it completely and explain itself to it without losing any time. A story is different. It does not expend itself. It preserves and concentrates its strength and is capable of releasing it even after a long time." Explanation is cosubstantial with information and helps to avoid the sharp edges which the event seems to present at the moment of its accommodation to law. The novelty of news always brings with it a breath of relative wonder, which the accompanying explanation smoothly helps to dissipate. This does not happen in storytelling: "Actually, it is half the art of storytelling to keep a story free from explanation as one reproduces it. . . . The most extraordinary things, marvelous things, are related with the greatest accuracy, but the psychological connection of the events is not forced on the reader. It is left up to him to interpret things the way he understands them, and thus the narrative achieves an amplitude that information lacks."

This is also the root of the essential *ambiguity* of all storytelling, which we will have occasion to treat at length when we speak of *Treasure Island*. For two fundamental reasons, true storytelling is always ambiguous: because no necessary law exhausts the inexplicable concreteness of its outlines and because it is really completed only in the innerness of the listener who accepts it, just as that half ring or that fragment of map acquires meaning only in the presence of the person who brings to it the missing piece. This is why the storyteller flees as from the plague from psychological analysis, in which the novel often finds abundant nourishment. The psychological novel gleefully accepts the fact that innerness is subject to a necessary law but never succeeds in finding it; the novel's purpose combines the drawbacks of the strictness to which it aspires and the dislocation which it in fact achieves. Borges has expressed it very wittily: "The typical 'psychological' novel tends to be formless. The Russians and the Russians' disciples have demonstrated *ad nauseam* that nobody is impossible: those who commit suicide because they are so happy, those who kill out of benevolence, persons who adore each other to the point of separating forever, accusers who act out of passion or humility. . . . That total Freedom is equivalent to total disorder."[5] The odd thing is that here disorder is induced by the exorbitant desire for precision. Really, psychology is that from which innerness is totally absent, precisely because it aspires only to confine that innerness. That is why Benjamin states that "there is nothing that commends a story to memory more effectively than that chaste compactness which precludes psychological analysis."

When I referred above to the community where storytelling takes place, in contrast to the solitude in which the novel moves,

I might have alluded to the relationship of these two very different conditions with memory.

It has seldom been realized that the listener's naïve relationship to the storyteller is controlled by his interest in retaining what he is told. The cardinal point for the unaffected listener is to assure himself of the possibility of reproducing the story. Memory is the epic faculty *par excellence*. Only by virtue of a comprehensive memory can epic writing absorb the course of events on the one hand and, with the passing of these, make its peace with the power of death on the other.

The novel, however, is unrepeatable; a juice distilled in a transference to pure individuality, its masturbatory privateness does not permit that status of paradigm which is what memory seizes upon in order to guarantee repetition. The specific factor in storytelling is to suppose that each man resembles all men more than that imprecise, vague ghost that we call "he himself." This conception does not do away with individual peculiarity, for it is precisely in being individually peculiar that all men resemble each other; but it guarantees the transmissibility of experience and the general validity of the foundation of things, which otherwise would get bogged down in the pure innovation that invalidates the entire past and compromises the entire future. This last is more in accord with the general fidgetiness of our present-day sensibility, so that the aspirations of storytelling are more and more alien to us even when they are not suspect.

In that repetition we struggle to achieve, what are we trying to bring back? The despotic power of feudal lords, the obscurantism of magicians and bishops, the periods when mace and sword were the only guarantees of survival? This is what happens when we try to read repetition with the crooked lines of our linear time; what threatens to return is what we are most afraid of, history, whose repetition would change our more or less useless efforts toward "progress" into the painful incline up which Sisyphus unavailingly and ceaselessly toils. But the repetition sought by storytelling is inscribed in the cyclical time of myths: what returns is not history but poetry, creation. In storytelling what return are the pillars of our human condition: the encounter with sea and forest, a definition of ourselves with respect to animals, the adolescent's initiation into love and war, the triumph of cunning over strength, the reinvention of solidarity, the rewards of boldness and mercy. And also the marks of time's claws, the separation of those who love each other, exploitation and usury, feeble senility, death. Repetition, to which Kierkegaard dedicated his most impassioned pages, is the full restitution of what we have possessed, the restoration, intact, of the strength we have spent in combat lost or won, the reconstruction of the world, the abolition of all that is irremediable. Storytelling is the possibility of reinventing reality, of recovering possibilities when we are faced with difficulties or adversities. When it loses its regenerative function, which is directly connected with that substantive hope we have already discussed, storytelling withers. The decline of storytelling is one of the innumerable present-day symptoms of the decline of memory, some of whose quite obvious aspects are the impoverishment of study of classical languages or of history courses in secondary education.

Let us continue our descent into the center of storytelling, following the footsteps of that W.B. who fills the role of Arne Saknussemm. I warn you that we are now very close to the deepest area of this investigation. And at the end of our *descensus ad inferos* we also find the contrast with the novel which has accompanied us throughout the journey. The novel is built upon the dissociation between life and meaning, between the temporal and the essential, as Lukács tells us. The reconciliation of the two extremes, or their becoming bogged down in the irreconcilable, can be achieved only in the novelist's attempt to encompass all of their peculiarity: "The 'meaning of life' is really the center about which the novel moves. But the quest for it is no more than the initial expression of perplexity with which its reader sees himself living this written life. Here 'meaning of life'—there 'moral of the story': with these slogans novel and story confront each other, and from them the totally different historical co-ordinates of these art forms may be discerned."

We already understand, in some sense, what is meant when the "meaning of life" is discussed; the allusion is to the wrenching confrontation between the character's innerness and the pressures to which the outside world subjects him, together with the vague demand—so often frustrated—for a perspective, there at the boundaries of the stream of life, which will bring about an adequate harmonization. But this "moral of the story," applied to storytelling, is not at all obvious and requires elucidation. Had not Michael Innes said that the story has nothing to do with values? But not even blood-and-thunder stories, not even dreams, lack valuation. Yet more, they are the moments of full evaluative choice, of confrontation, the triumph and defeat of tendencies from which arises the hierarchy of values. There, the respective prestige of cunning versus nobility, the demands of strength and mercy, the exaltation of friendship, and the bracing tonic of solitude, confront each other. In the vigorous and ambiguous moment that storytelling relates, we are present at the genealogical origin of morals. But not of moralizing, and this is the crucial point. In storytelling, for the hero—that is, the one who selects his actions with the most integrity and grace—everything turns out well, strength and victory; even if he is defeated and annihilated, like Sandokan at the end of his saga on the deck of *King of the Sea*, his downfall becomes a poetic triumph more worthy than his enemies' victory. In exactly the same way, evil, weakness, and defeat cannot be discerned in his enemies. In storytelling values really count; they are not imposed in the name of any external demand. Nobody moralizes, but everybody performs moral actions. The reader knows that nothing bad can happen to the protagonist, even though he may perish, and some see this as a sign of laughable ingenuousness. But no; it is a noble and generous ingenuousness, born free, which still does not separate the good from the triumph of good, nor evil from the defeat of evil, and makes the hero advance secure and invulnerable into the very heart of hell, proving even there, when all is said and done, that the good is more practical, truer, the only thing that can really be counted on, and that not even death can give the lie to such dazzling proof.

In storytelling the protagonist is always a chosen vessel; but he is chosen because he has chosen well. In storytelling morality is not forcibly pulled out of shape, nor is it confused with the resentful sneer against greatness that is not shared. The hero triumphs because he is faithful, but he is faithful above all else to his vocation for triumph; faithful to his origin, to his curiosity, to his strength, to his independence, to what he really is. The hero is the one who remembers himself.

In *Poetry and Truth* Goethe speaks of a certain French captain who, according to the councilor of state, had a passion for meditation without any real capacity for thought. This captain was obsessed by a single idea, to which he returned interminably; he maintained that all virtue in the world sprang from a good memory and all vice from forgetfulness. Goethe comments, in one of his so-frequent disagreeable asides, that the captain "maintained this theory with much ingenuity, for anything can be maintained when you permit yourself to use words quite vaguely, now in a wider, now in a narrower, sense, and to vary them now by a closer, now by a more remote application."[6] However, I think that this thought of the captain's is at least as good as the best of Goethe's thoughts. Storytelling is based precisely on bestowing virtue on the one with the best memory and condemning every vice as a form of forgetfulness or, better still, every form of forgetting as a vice. The hero moves in that narrow and dangerous fringe where whoever forgets who he is and where he is going, perishes. And perishes without honor. In the tale of the three brothers who go one after another to the castle to rescue the princess, the first two do not dare to tread on the path of gems and diamonds, while the third, who does not forget why he is going there, tramples them without more ado. Or in Ruskin's tale *The King of the Golden River*, the two older brothers wind up turned to stone because, although they remember very well the gold they have gone to seek, they forget the even older, fundamental need to give water to the thirsty. What storytelling reminds us of, virtuously, is that there is no dissociation between innerness and the outside world, between life and meaning: that is precisely the "moral of the story." Coming after the widespread predominance of forgetting, the novel gropes in search of a reconciliation whose very presence is a proof of its impossibility.

In the last resort it can be said that the novel is oriented

toward death, while storytelling serves as orientation in life.
He who seeks the meaning of life can find it only in death; in
death innerness and outerness are at last reconciled in an im-
pregnable unity. The novelist traverses the length of life's path
and places himself at the end of it, to see his protagonist coming;
he tells his whole story from the necessary foreshortening of
hindsight. No one is happy until the end of life, the novel tells
us, nor radically unhappy either, for if there is some meaning
it will gush out with the last breath, like the stroke that separates
the sums to be added from the final result of the addition. Only
at the end can a balance be struck, can one be understood at
last, in the only way that the life of the isolated individual can
be understood, in a sudden act of remembrance by the crepus-
cular light of death. They are the crowded memories of past
existence that assault drowning men's last instants, according
to legend.

In this light, how complete and pregnant with meaning death
appears, contrasted with the meaninglessness of life! Benjamin
reminds us of Moritz Heimann's dictum that a man who dies
at the age of thirty-five is at every point of his life a man who
dies at the age of thirty-five. The stamp of death marks
backward.

The "meaning of his life" is revealed only in his death. But the reader
of a novel actually does look for human beings from whom he derives
the "meaning of life." Therefore he must, in one way or another,
know in advance that he will share their experience of death: if need
be their figurative death—the end of the novel—but preferably their
actual one. How do the characters make him understand that death
is already waiting for them—a very definite death and at a very definite
place? That is the question which feeds the reader's consuming interest
in the events of the novel.

The last page is equivalent to the last breath and marks the
beginning of meaning, whose vector points backward. That is
why the novel is a great *Christian* invention, arising from the
bourgeois laicization of the lives of medieval saints, in which
the last ordeal of martyrdom, beatitude, or repentance illuminated in each case a story that had no other meaning than to

prepare this salvation-giving death. The two earliest novels tell the story of a saint and martyr, Don Quixote, and of an anchorite, Robinson Crusoe. Death, the last page, confers a sufficient dimension on both lives and rescues them, in some sense, from themselves: the madness of Don Quixote's life ends in the sanity of his death, Crusoe's paradisiacal solitude ends in the teeming intrigues of a new colony. The meaning that death gives to both lives is, significantly, disillusionment. In the end death knows only how to give the lie to life; unlucky is the man who hopes to be confirmed by death, the man who wagers on it in the hope of meaning! Because of this the novel is a despairing genre, in contrast to storytelling as a hopeful and hope-giving one. But despair is an attribute much more characteristic of the novel's reader than of the novel itself, for it is the reader's vitality which is truly involved: "What draws the reader to the novel is the hope of warming his shivering life with a death he reads about."

In storytelling, however, death is always present, authoritarianly present, we might say; but it is never necessary nor in any way a dispenser of meaning. Meaning is something that belongs to life, is life itself, and hence it is life that can confer meaning on death, never vice versa. Death is a silence, a blank space, which needs all the rest of the sphere of meaning to acquire intelligibility and excellence. The protagonist of a story that is told cannot hope for that vicarious death at the end of the story in order to finally understand himself, for the simple reason that storytelling never ends. As Benjamin would say, there is in fact no possible story in which the question, "And what happens next?" fails to have meaning. The reader will observe that this question is precisely the one that never applies to a well-written novel. No matter how much theorizing there may be about the "open work," the novel is the most closed genre there is, in which all the ends are tied up and firmly tied up, for precisely the last page (death) is the only absolutely indispensable page in the novel. And this means that death ends, but life goes on; note that we would not be able to say "death goes on." The formula that ends stories in German, Benjamin reminds us, is "and if they're not dead they live there still"—

a vagueness that not only emphasizes the narrative nonnecessity
of death, which appears as a possibility but not the only possibility, but also offers the possibility of taking up the story
again, twenty years later, say.[7] The Spanish formula is even
more life-enhancing: "Y fueron felices y comieron perdices"
[And they were happy and ate partridges]. Why not? The rhyme
is not forced but is a statement of the fact that happiness must
be intimately connected with things like eating partridges after
having had adventures. We will see something of this when we
discuss Tolkien. In both cases the end of the story opens onto
life, that is, onto the possibility of continuing to tell a story,
of repeating the story to others, of extracting practical advantage from what has been told. The initiatory and preparatory
nature of storytelling would be absurd if the story ended in
death. Basically, the person who comes to the end of a story
always has all of life ahead of him: to repeat the story, to live
it, to be happy and eat partridges or get ready to hear the next
story. In any case, death can neither confirm nor deny values
whose efficacy is affirmed specifically against death; not only
are they attitudes which do not expect death in order to acquire
meaning, they expect everything but death, in which meaning
itself is closed off and dissolves in a blind alley.

If light is shed on storytelling it does not come from ahead,
from that last moment by whose dark gleam the novel must
be read, but from behind, where experience waits and where
memory carries us back. Experience and memory form a combination with intertwined silhouettes that we call the mythic
world. It is a heavy burden for us, but it is the place to which
scrabbling in the genealogy of our values—that is, our incorruptible actions—leads us. Storytelling teaches us how to locate
ourselves in relation to that mythic world. It does not preach
to us about how to "overcome" it, in the modern rationalist
way—let us pass over the fact that storytelling belongs to wisdom, to the epic side of truth—but it does preach

how mankind "acts dumb" toward the myth; in the figure of the
youngest brother it shows us how one's chances increase as the mythical primitive times are left behind; in the figure of the man who sets
out to learn what fear is it shows us that the things we are afraid of
can be seen through; in the figure of the wiseacre it shows us that the

questions posed by the myth are simple-minded, like the riddle of the Sphinx; in the shape of the animals which come to the aid of the child in the fairy tale it shows that nature not only is subservient to the myth, but much prefers to be aligned with man.

But observe that this happens without breaking away from the mythic world. Enlightenment—represented in a good proportion of novels—cures us of the marvel of our origins by dissipating all marvels, and assuring us that we no longer have anything to do with the dark shadow of the past; from this world, as we know, we are condemned to await from the even more gloomy shadow of death the final accolade that will confirm us in a reality which, in that last instant, we simultaneously win and lose.

Storytelling, on the other hand, reaffirms an affiliation whose scope it makes perfectly clear. The rigidity and remoteness of myth, characteristic of one of its aspects, succeed in erasing the passages by which it comes close to us, making it seem strange and even hostile to innerness: storytelling casts light on our link with that primordial area, dissipating the sensation of alienation and oppression that may arise from it. By means of the story, we know to what point myth preserves our freedom of initiative and is familiar to the foundations of our innerness; in a word, it gives us back memory. When the sclerosis of myth threatens to end its potential vitality, storytelling reconstitutes it on a much fresher and more stimulating plane, less connected with remote origins and more deeply rooted in the richer form of everydayness.

Sometimes the humorous or irreverent attitude toward the mythic world adopted by the story's protagonist is the expression of a profound pity toward the liberating essence of myth. It arose to free man from blind necessity and make him confide in the limitless divine powers that he shares and in the institutions that his freedom creates. But when the divine or the institutional adopt the heavy face of need to oppress man's valiant heart, man must combat myth with myth and tell himself new legends about his courage, his skill, and his independence.

The wisest thing—so the fairy tale taught mankind in olden times, and teaches children to this day—is to meet the forces of the mythical world with cunning and with high spirits. (This is how the fairy tale polarizes *Mut*, courage, dividing it dialectally into *Untermut*, that is, cunning, and *Übermut*, high spirits.) The liberating magic which the fairy tale has at its disposal does not bring nature into play in a mythical way, but points to its complicity with liberated man. A mature man feels this complicity only occasionally, that is, when he is happy; but the child first meets it in fairy tales, and it makes him happy.

The important word here is *complicity*. By means of it the opposition between innerness and outerness ceases, without that agreement's having to pay with a tribute of forced submission. As José Bergamín says shrewdly, "Man is free when he places himself in agreement with the gods instead of obeying them."[8] The deepest meaning of storytelling is precisely the proof of that agreement, which is consolidated in the profound intensity of the value of life, and is maintained in the secret palpitations of man's happiness or in children's joy.

Thus far we have followed more or less loosely the article by Walter Benjamin, which has saved us from many gropings and has offered us fundamental ideas. Benjamin ends his essay with a few words on the storyteller himself, of whom he can say, "His gift is the ability to relate his life; his distinction, to be able to tell his entire life." And finally, "The storyteller is the figure in which the righteous man encounters himself." Thus is beatified the man who gathers the energy to raise his voice and begin the story. The righteous man is the one who tells the tale in two senses: the one who recounts and the one who counts. We need not go back to the respect that in primitive cultures attaches to the storyteller, the master of stories, to establish the unbreakable tie which unites moral preeminence with the storyteller's function. It is enough to look into a child's eyes while we are telling him a story. In those eyes we read a hope that everyone will get his deserts, not as a purely external determination, which falls like a cold shower on the characters' shrinking shoulders, but as an inner fire that goes on spreading and reaffirming itself in the marvelous chain of adventures. To risk telling a story is to decide to institute an order of things to which only the storyteller's rectitude responds; that is, his fidelity to experience and to memory. When one begins to tell a story one must be ready to tell all of it; an interminable cycle is begun, which the question, "And then what happened?" can prolong endlessly. But the storyteller does not have the right to reserve part of his existence for himself—or for silence—since the same demand for rectitude on which his tale is based confirms him in a perfect discursive transparency. Justice is what can always be recognized; it is the tellable par excellence. The storyteller swears by his own life that he will not lie, or, what is still more important, belie himself; and that is precisely what counts, what matters. No risk is greater for the one who chooses it, nor more necessary for the community which expects everything from that connection.

Earlier I alluded in passing to the present-day decrease in the taste for storytelling, a taste considered sufficient motive to accuse someone of childishness. Those who still like stories read them as if they were unsuccessful novels, frustrated efforts that have not succeeded in making their purposes explicit and that have sheltered the confusion of their parables in the kindergarten. It may well be that such a shelter is an exile, or even a prison. Read as if they were novels, the inadequacy of stories is immediately soothing; the peremptory obviousness of their expedients condemns them either to the venial or the allegorical category, and none of their demands is great enough to be disturbing. Perhaps they require something that no one is capable of giving, but they do it in a style nobody feels obliged to accept; one can take it or leave it and everybody is happy. So children and adolescents are transitory sufferers from a condition no one could sustain without being considered unhealthy in some way. Storytelling belongs to them, forms the furniture of their world along with masturbation, acne, and religious anxieties. It is a period of imagination run riot, unjustified longings, in which loneliness and friendship are compatible, even complementary, passions. It is the time when we read, listen, and yearn. And from that long-past time in our lives a sort of impassioned buzzing reaches our ears, which only Freud dared to examine and then not exactly with happy results. At that time reading is, as we seem to remember with a sort of shamed shudder, an overpowering, wild pleasure. Fortunately the stage does not last long, and afterward we can never again read like that, which keeps books from being a problem for us and makes them compatible with the division of labor and resignation. It is a merciful transmutation of our longings into the realm of necessity.

And yet when we are older, almost mature, we sometimes return to the forbidden sphere of stories, where jungles full of gleaming eyes and the ghostships of our childhood still lie in wait. We descend to our souls' misty homeland, anesthetized by grownupness, swaddled in that sensation of controlled escape that comes over us on Saturday afternoons. We raise like a banner a word that for some is censure, for others an incentive, and for everyone a proper defense against the fatal poison of nostalgia: escape. But, all of a sudden, escape from what, and to go where? The stereotyped replies are: to escape from reality so as to go to the limbo of what cannot be (what could never be, what can no longer be, what cannot be yet, or what cannot be for me). It is not impossible to find a flaw in this unremarkable idea.

Like all abstractions that are cloudy and contradictory, but disappointing, the word *reality* enjoys great prestige among persons of common sense. It is an idea connected with frequency; a woman selling chestnuts in Chamberí is more real than a pirate because I have seen many women selling chestnuts but never a pirate, for it is more usual to see women selling chestnuts than pirates, or because women selling chestnuts happen to be closer to me than pirates. This form of realism resembles nothing so much as laziness, which makes one prefer the bad film that is showing just around the corner to the good one we have to go downtown for. But, says the scoffer, is it not pitifully childish to enjoy what is far away just because it is far away and the unusual because it is unusual? Of course not. Farawayness and strangeness are aesthetic categories no more (or no less) childish than the rest, and we are spurred by those categories to undertake journeys and come to know landscapes and temples whose chief merit lies precisely in remoteness and strangeness. The person who lives at the foot of the Acropolis or across from the Grand Canyon of the Colorado enjoys these marvels in a very different way from the pilgrim who comes from far-off lands to contemplate them, and who in every case adds to his enjoyment that other, incomparable enjoyment of being a pilgrim. The joy of recognition is very great, but that of seeing for the first time what one has so often dreamed about is no less great, and obviously the first depends on the second.

On the other hand, if we entrench ourselves on the very lowest level of philistinism, all fiction and all chronicles are equally unreal: Fafnir the dragon does not exist but neither does Madame Bovary. That some find the latter more acceptable, and some the former, can be a question of education and even, perhaps, of metabolism. If we argue that the case of the lady who is unfaithful to her husband is more frequent than that of a dragon guarding a treasure, we can answer in two ways: first, that between a lady who is unfaithful to her husband and Madame Bovary there is the same impossible resemblance as that which equates the lizard at the entrance to his nest with Fafnir; second, that ladies who cheat on their husbands are a false invention of dragons, put forth so that no one will dare to go and look for treasure. In any case, not to credit what this world has decided to proclaim as "real" seems to be in itself the primary and healthiest vocation of rebels.

But the label of "escapism" that clings to stories has, at bottom, a certain connection with what is considered to be this genre's secret sin: its artificiality. It has been said that they are tales which seek to produce an effect, not to reproduce the supreme limpidity of life "as it really is." The novel, conversely, tries to resemble that mirror placed alongside the road, to use Stendhal's moving and elusive figure of speech. The key to the novel's whole ambition resides in the word *naturalism*, which designates not only a particular way of writing novels but the function of novel-writing itself.

Storytelling belongs to the sphere of innerness and religion; from the very beginning it is a pure, spiritual effort, an artifice. The novel, on the other hand, arises in the sphere of the natural sciences and tries to be a spontaneous reflection of the real, naturalism. One of our contemporaries who has most success-

fully thought about literature, Jorge Luis Borges, expresses it
like this:

The "psychological" novel also wants to be a "realistic" novel; it
prefers that we forget its nature as a verbal artifice and makes of all
vain precision (or of all languid vagueness) a new realistic touch. There
are pages, there are whole chapters of Marcel Proust which are not
convincing as inventions; and without realizing that we are doing so,
we resign ourselves to them just as we resign ourselves to the boring
and futile parts of each day. The adventure novel, however, does not
attempt to be a transcription of reality: it is an artificial object in which
there is no room for any unjustified part.[9]

This artificiality of the story is based on its decidedly anthropocentric nature. The universe of tales has its center in the
human spirit, and everything turns on its conflicts, its creations,
and its aims; the novel, however, is a de-centered, ex-centric
genre that in some sense mimics the mechanical unfolding of
material forces, which lack aims and are either hostile to or
ignorant of human aims. Storytelling tries for an effect, of
course; it does not aspire to simple contemplation or analysis
of the given. In this sense it occupies the same position with
respect to the novel as ethics with respect to science. Today,
everything that most urgently calls us to evaluation seems suspicious, and with good reason; the novel adjusts itself more
successfully to our tastes with its simple descriptions of una-
dorned events, among which values appear as so many more
subjective facts, needing skillful dissection like other facts.

The world of storytelling strikes us as excessively free, for
all the external circumstances act only as moral problems which
can be solved by the choice of the proper action; but they lack
that inert material cumbrousness that characterizes the obstacles
in our daily life, which the novel, however, successfully reproduces. Nevertheless, it is necessary to remind ourselves here
that the storyteller always tells the story from the hero's viewpoint, and that from that perspective reality is essentially a free
field for the righteous man's activities. The hero is not an op-
timist, but a man of action; the storyteller is not unaware of
the weight of the inert, but trusts in the energy he knows how

to choose. If the bureaucratic serenity of the hard-working soul, whose only moral consolation is its condition as victim, requires it, we can give the name of "escapism" to that careless confidence with which the storyteller, when he takes up the tale, installs himself immediately and without apology on a victorious plane.

Where can we escape to? For if it were really possible to leave this world for another and better one, I can't see any reason not to. The question lies in what Paul Éluard condensed in a happy formula: "There are other worlds, but they are in this one." Storytelling does not abandon the plane of the strictest reality, though it may be only because that is impossible by definition: we give the name of reality to what we cannot leave behind, to what always catches up with us. But flight does not enter the storyteller's plans either; we began by defining him as the one who comes from far away. The storyteller does not go away but in fact has been there and returned. To carry things a bit further, he has come back from everything; this is why he begins everything at the beginning, unhurriedly, constructing another world piece by piece but so that his hearers can win, as he has, the right to reside in this world. They say that Shakespeare was very good in the role of the ghost of Hamlet's father; his soul, aflame with the living of stories, took pleasure in that veiled figure which returns from very far away to uncover—recall—for his son a truth that he knows already, and which Hamlet must repeat in his turn as drama, only to suffer it later as revenge.

# 2

# A TREASURE OF
# AMBIGUITY

My youthful eyes rejoiced in the infinite sea . . .
From a recording of Robert Louis Stevenson, *Treasure Island*

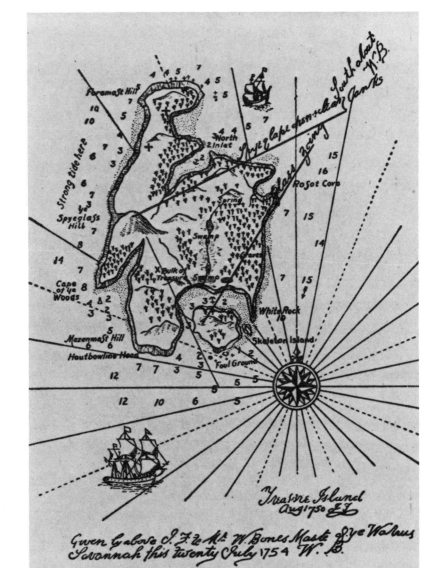

THE PUREST PIECE of storytelling I know, the one that most perfectly combines the initiatory and the epic, shadows of violence, and the macabre with the incomparable splendor of triumphant audacity, the scent of seagoing adventure—which is always the most perfect, the most absolute adventure—with the subtle complexity of a boy's first and decisive moral choice; in short, the most beautiful story that has ever been told me, is *Treasure Island*. Rarely does the year pass that I do not reread it at least once; and more than six months never pass without having thought about it or dreamed of it. It is not easy to put one's finger on the source of this book's inexhaustible magic, for like all good stories it aspires only to be told and retold, not explained or commented on. Mind you, I am not saying that it is impossible to comment on it or explain it; I am only stating that this is not what it aspires to, what it requires of its hearer's or reader's generosity. Yet nothing is simpler than to point out several of its obvious partial charms: its impeccable sobriety of style, the narrative rhythm that seems to sum up all perfection in the art of storytelling, the vigorous depiction of its characters, the shrewd complexity of an extremely simple plot.

A first reading might give the impression that it is the story of one fabulous figure, John Silver; but then we notice that the really disconcerting character, the hero of the tale in every sense of the word, is Jim Hawkins, whose view of Silver is what constitutes the latter's whole enigma. It is tempting to compare the relationship of the *Hispaniola*'s cabin boy and its cook with that which connects Ishmael and Ahab; but it would be a mistake to think of them as similar. It is true that both Ishmael and Jim are forced to make the fundamental moral choice when they confront an exhibition of untamable energy from the two ferocious cripples who threaten them; it is true that both Ahab and Silver utterly crush the soft substance of everyday corporate morality, demonstrating the invulnerable reality of authentic free will; and it is no less true that both succeed in terrorizing and repelling the civilized, almost mother-ridden Ishmael and Jim. But the positive aspect of the comparison ends here, for the reactions of Ishmael and Jim are diametrically opposite when they are faced with the challenge of their overpowering tempters Ishmael chooses sides against Ahab from the very first moment; his fascinated attraction to the *Pequod*'s captain is based precisely on the nostalgic feeling of knowing that he is everything Ahab is not; Ishmael loves the sea as a terrible, though exciting, alternative to his real everyday world, the land; Ahab knows nothing of the land, to which he does not belong; and he *is* the sea, the white monster and the deep abyss. In Ahab's ocean, Ishmael disappears; he comes to the surface only for an instant, to recount his anti-Ahabian joy in fondling the sperm whale's delicious softness; when he finally reappears it is because Ahab, the whale, and all that they represent have disappeared in the welcome blackness of memory, out of which he begins to tell the tale: "Call me Ishmael. . . ." But Jim accepts Silver's challenge and fights on the pirate's own ground; in fact, as the one-legged cook reminds him, he becomes the only real buccaneer in addition to Silver—the vigorous whelp of an extinct breed. This is why Jim does not weaken when he enters the pirates' dangerous terrain—the sea, the gloomy, swampy island, the schooner's secret depths—but acquires more and more strength, changes from narrator into protagonist, tells the story to himself (while Ishmael tells it to Ahab) and at the end of the book splits in two: part of him, part of the treasure, goes with Silver and part remains with the representatives of the established order. And there is more, for Jim's last thought at the end of the novel is for the bar silver that still remains on the island, and which, as he coolly says, "certainly . . . shall lie there for me." A dangerous coolness, and profoundly ambiguous, like everything else in this disconcerting story.

This radical ambiguity is the secret, or the treasure if you like, of this peerless tale. The many-faceted world of adolescence, that is, the world of the moment immediately previous to the invention of necessity, here achieves its finest literary crystallization (leaving out Henry James' *The Turn of the Screw*, if you wish). The unhesitating and definite judgment which morality always thinks it is ready to dictate has never been so hopelessly frustrated.

John Silver, hypocrite, murderer, and traitor, struggles to take possession of a treasure which belongs much more to the pirates who had striven and suffered for that gold than to the prosperous adventurers who are trying to take it over thanks to fortuitous circumstances. His attitude toward Jim is always perfectly loyal, even when he deceives him, just as the serpent's was toward Adam and Eve; and finally, Silver saves Jim's life, the murderer's and thief's life Jim has decided to create for himself on the pirates' isle.

The intriguing figure of Jim Hawkins piles up endless ambivalences; a spy who sees and hears everything, he passes from one side to another in a rapid and equivocal kind of traffic, incapable of staying quietly in one camp or the other, faithful only to himself as a fugitive, an infiltrator. His apparently frail figure is revealed at every turn as the strongest one in the story, the cleverest and most implacable, but also as obviously childish; he is the catalyst of the action, the one who throws the dice anew every time the story bogs down in apparent equilibrium, the inexorable inciter of adventure.

And what shall we say of other, minor paradoxes, such as Ben Gunn, that ragged millionaire, a repentant pirate, the scarecrow figure who is inescapably master of the situation? He is the most inept and ridiculous of all Flint's henchmen, but the only one who can pass himself off as Flint, as a spectral voice among the trees, because he is the owner of the pirates' hoard. Captain Flint's true heir is this pitiable ghost, whom his companions do not respect living or dead! And those most worthy squires Trelawney, Dr. Livesey, and the others reveal a suspicious talent for deception and for alliances that are more opportunist than opportune, in addition to other traits whose morality is decidedly pragmatic, such as their truly buccaneerish greed for the island's treasures.

Although in the strict sense it cannot be said that anyone steps out of his role (except Jim?), and all the characters more or less respect the convention of their respective positions in life, the course of the story implicitly undermines the confidence each character has in his own logic. All of them know how to make good speeches rationalizing their behavior, but from time to time a small revealing sigh slips out, such as that moment when Trelawney, at the beginning of the treasure voyage, confesses that he admired old Flint and "was sometimes proud he was an Englishman."

The Spanish word *peripecia*, a sudden reversal of circumstances, comes from the Greek *peripeteia*, an unexpected turning of tables. In this etymological sense, the reversals of Jim and John Silver are truly dizzying. Jim changes, almost unconsciously, from the good son of a modest family, helping his parents to run the family business, into first the confidant and then the legatee of an old pirate from the great Flint's crew. However, he is the accomplice of another buccaneer, a blind man, who delivers to the first pirate the "black spot," a buccaneer-style ultimatum, and the way he collects the inheritance which implicitly belongs to him rather closely resembles theft. From there he goes on to be the one who sets off the expedition by discovering the map and making it public; the complete break with his former life is made clear when he returns to the inn to say goodbye to his mother, and finds that she has brought in a boy of his own age to help her in the work of the place. This intruder who is occupying his niche in normal life definitely uproots him, propels him toward adventure. He becomes the *Hispaniola*'s cabin boy and the scullion of Silver the cook—becomes his friend and faithful listener to Silver's tales of pirates, in which Jim's own experiences are prefigured. But he is the one who listens to and warns of the buccaneers' plot, crouched in the apple barrel as if he were the ship's good spirit, a seagoing—and quiet—poltergeist.

As soon as they reach the treasure island, Jim goes into a frenzy of escapes. First he jumps into Silver's boat even though he has discovered his plot, thus escaping from those who presumably are on his side (Trelawney, Livesey, etc.). As soon as he sets foot on land he also flees from Silver and the rest of the pirates to wander alone on the island. He encounters the hermit Ben Gunn, whose lack of confidence in this disconcerting fugitive is matched by the reader's excited uneasiness in the face of such confusing behavior. He again joins his former companions, the "good guys," in the old stockade, fights along with them like one of their own, and again surreptitiously abandons them when night falls. And what is his objective? To take over the *Hispaniola*! The innkeeper's boy, the cabin boy, the spy, the friend of Bill Bones and John Silver, now finally turned into a pirate, sets out to board the schooner. And he wins it, steers it to a distant cove, and is its commander; now he is Captain Jim Hawkins. Of the Royal Navy? Despite the fact that he strikes the black flag, his actions are more those of a buccaneer than of an officer of His Gracious Majesty; let us leave him as a pirate, to be fair to him. In any case, he shows himself to be an energetic captain, who does not hesitate to kill the mutinous Israel Hands in order to maintain control in the conquered ship. Now where is the timid, pious servant of the *Admiral Benbow*? He returns to the stockade and by sheer chance finds himself in the midst of the pirate camp, again John Silver's accomplice and confidant. Next morning Dr. Livesey bitterly reproaches him for his behavior and urges Jim to escape with him, despite his having given Silver his word of honor not to do so. But Jim refuses, he *cannot* leave; he, who unhesitatingly breaks all the promises of obedience he had made to Captain Smollett and Trelawney, gives unbreakable precedence to the oath sworn to a pirate, thus implicitly respecting the *omertà* of the Brothers of the Coast. In the end it is with John Silver that he sets off in search of the treasure, and it is legitimate to ask what would have happened if it had been the pirate who had found Flint's gold; in any case, the patient greed of Ben Gunn, the marooned pirate, had already placed it in safety, perhaps preventing Jim from doing another about-face.

On his side, the figure of John Silver suffers no fewer sudden reversals. The first has occurred before the story's beginning and has carried him from quartermaster of Flint's *Walrus* to innkeeper of *The Spyglass* in Bristol, as we learn when we listen with Jim from inside the apple barrel. From there he becomes cook of the *Hispaniola*, an "official" job which he carries on simultaneously with his role as leader of the pirates' mutiny that is being planned on the schooner. Implacable murderer of the sailors loyal to Captain Smollett, no sooner does he reach the island than he assumes the title of "Captain" Silver, being, together with Smollett himself and Jim, the third person of this rank to appear in the novel at one point or another.[1] He soon changes roles, from the vicious attacker of the stockade to the one responsible for converting it into a refuge, leaving the "good guys" the role of marauders without a camp. His ambiguous actions, as he protects and uses Jim, place him at odds with the rest of the pirates, who send him the black spot; but he smothers the rebellion by showing the treasure map which the "good guys" have given him with suspicious ease. Does he really believe that he has a chance to find Flint's wealth, or does he perform the ritual of search to the very end as a means of escaping from his dangerous and disillusioned companions, whom he leads into a trap? Certainly, in the final ambush he cooperates with the "good guys" by killing the ringleader of the recent rebellion against his authority. Finally, Silver quietly rejoins the winning group and responds to Smollett's question with "Come back to my dooty, sir," to which the legitimate captain either cannot or will not reply. Completely transformed, he even joins in celebrating their departure from the island like one more member of the victorious group: "And there was Silver, sitting back almost out of the firelight, but eating heartily, prompt to spring forward when anything was wanted, even joining quietly in our laughter—the same bland, polite, obsequious seaman of the voyage out."

He still gets a chance to show one last side when he flees with a modest part of the treasure, thanks to Ben Gunn's complicity and the tacit compliance of the rest of the "good guys," who are happy to be free of him and the knotty problem of bringing him to justice. In the last chapter there is a particularly impressive moment when, before they finally embark from the island, the night breeze brings to Dr. Livesey and Jim a noise of laughter or distant shrieking. It is the surviving pirates, wandering ghostlike on the island, already mingling with the other ghosts of Flint's crew. Their cries are the result of despairing drunkenness or the delirium of fever, and Dr. Livesey feels pity for them and even wonders if it is not his duty to offer them the services of his profession. Silver, very much at home in his new role, as he had been in all the previous ones, dissuades him from doing so, for those men, he says, can neither keep their

word nor believe that anyone else can. Livesey replies indig-
nantly that his case is not exactly different, to which Silver
makes no reply, though evidence of the difference leaps to the
eye: Silver is there and not with the ghosts, which proves that
he knows very well which promises he must keep. His old
associates must also have arrived at this same conclusion, as is
significantly proved by the bullet that a vengeful pirate fires on
the departing schooner, which passes a few inches over Silver's
head.

But what particularly intrigues the thoughtful reader, the one
who reads the book for the second time (and who is not always
the best reader), is the relationship between Jim and Silver. If
some psychoanalyst has studied this novel—and I don't know
whether one has—he would not have failed to notice that the
story begins with the death of Jim's father and ends with the
disappearance of Silver, who acts as a father image for the boy
throughout the novel. Seen in these terms, the whole story can
be understood as a meditation on orphanhood, or, if you like,
as that acceptance of solitude which marks the adolescent's entrance into adulthood. Silver, unworthy but stimulating, dangerous but also a helper if his aid can be gained, such a virtuoso
of hypocrisy that he succeeds in making it an unusual form of
frankness, is the father who shows how to renounce parents,
the father whose astonishing strength and freedom establishes
a law which refutes all attempts at legislation. Only by demonstrating in his own person the most radical independence and
the most unconditional courage does Jim win the right to be
helped by Silver and to help him; the strongest man sells the
right to his complicity by courage and freedom. But I do not
want to speak in a language that is not mine, and so I leave the
familiar metaphors for the professionals of such pastimes. I
would rather couch the question in moral terms, if the adjective
serves. Jim has to decide whether his field of activity is that of
the pirates, or, as a child would brutally put it, whether John
Silver is good or bad. And there is no use here in retreating to
the holier-than-thou superiority of adult relativism, which
knows already that it all depends, mind you, and that all of us
are both good and bad. For we are inside the greatest adventure

of all, among pirates and in mortal danger, with an incalculable treasure at stake, and we must make the right choice or perish in the attempt. Jim is aware that there are two ways of doing things, two opposite ways—Captain Smollett's and Captain Silver's—and that both ways, if the cards are played right, can offer unsuspected resources of strength and admirable victories. All his initial education, all the language he has been given, inclines him to respect and imitate Captain Smollett's way and not to seek salvation outside it; but, and this is the story's hidden plot, events point him toward the pirates' world, offering him the profound temptation of piracy; that is, the suggestion that, to win a real buccaneer's treasure, one must in some sense become a buccaneer. At this point John Silver, master buccaneer, appears and gratuitously offers him his irresistible lesson. Smollett's way does not lead to the treasure, for he has no sympathetic relationship with the treasure; Silver's way is the constant promise of it. In the end Silver escapes with the most precious part of the treasure, that is, with his spirit and panache—these are riches that no one can steal from the pirate. There is a crucial moment in the story when Jim and Silver are as honest with each other as their respective roles permit. When Jim climbs into the stockade after hiding the *Hispaniola* and falls unexpectedly into the pirates' hands, he believes himself lost and blurts out all his activities against them—his spying in the barrel, stealing the schooner, and so on—and admits to having played a leading role in the action at every moment, offering with breathtaking audacity to intercede for them if they spare his life. Then he turns to Silver and says,

"And now, Mr. Silver, I believe you're the best man here, and if things go to the worst, I'll take it kind of you to let the doctor know the way I took it."

"I'll bear it in mind," said Silver, with an accent so curious that I could not, for the life of me, decide whether he were laughing at my request or had been favourably affected by my courage.

This short dialogue is particularly significant. Jim has just explained his piratical behavior, has ratified Silver's teachings, and asks him, the man most likely to understand him, to explain to the "good guys" the inevitability of that behavior in view of the enterprise they had undertaken. If one really wants to experience a search for treasure, then one must experience it as a pirate. Now Jim, who has sufficiently demonstrated his buccaneering aptitudes both to Silver and himself, has also really earned, and not in the form of resentment or timidity, the right to reject piracy, which is what he solemnly does at that moment, and even offers the possibility of repentance to his hearers. From that time onward Jim begins to disengage himself from the treasure, until his final declaration that nothing in the world would bring him back to seek the rest of the riches hidden on the island. His proving is over, his choice is made. Or is it? Because he still studies Silver to see if he is laughing at him or approves his actions; because, the next day, he will not escape with the doctor so as not to break his sworn word to the pirate; because, after all, what would have happened if John Silver had been the one to find the treasure? Neither Stevenson nor anyone else can know that; fortunately, the story has no other ending than the events themselves which form it, and which resist to the end any conclusive interpretation.

To summarize, I have read and still read *Treasure Island* as a reflection on audacity. Jim Hawkins is undoubtedly audacious from his first appearance in the novel, but left to himself he would not be capable of exploring all the aspects of his gift, especially that moment of transgression without which it cannot be said that true audacity exists. This is John Silver's virtue, to show audacity's *demonic* face to Jim. And there is no doubt that Jim takes full advantage of the lesson, recoiling from none of the violent, rapacious, or destructive aspects of demoniacal audacity. And this continues to the end, until his domesticated and soothing final return to the "good guys." This twist of the plot is also an audacious act, perhaps the greatest of the whole tale, the one that was being carefully prepared in all the previous reversals. In the end, is it not the demoniacal John Silver himself who teaches Jim the tactical virtues of a timely reunion with the side of the law? "Come back to my dooty, sir." Oh, the old fox! And what matchless audacity, what a splendid lesson in freedom! Desperate and disillusioned audacity of freedom!

Jim accepts the challenge like a true pirate, ready to go on to the end of the adventure. In a fight without quarter, by trickery and by death, he has won the ship, the island, and the treasure; now comes the most difficult test, the hour of renunciation, and in this predicament his audacity does not flag either. Now John Silver can disappear in the hurly-burly of the port, for the game has been played, and well played, to the very end. And so boldness has imposed its own order, and perhaps Jim will become a squire; but the dream, ah, the dream is uncontrollable. There another legend goes on uninterruptedly. There the waves break forever on the shores of the remote island, and the parrot voice of Flint's unquiet ghost keeps on crying "Pieces of eight! Pieces of eight!" as if it were calling us to new adventures.

# 3

## THE JOURNEY
## DOWNWARD

"Look, and look hard! You must take lessons in abysses."
Jules Verne, *A Journey to the Center of the Earth*

T HE INITIATORY NATURE of adventure novels whose plot consists of a journey is widely recognized even by critics who
most obstinately resist the mythologization of storytelling. In
fact, eighty percent of adventures either explicitly or implicitly
take the form of a journey, always easily interpretable as a series
of steps toward initiation. The pattern is obvious: the adolescent, still within the placental confines of the natural, receives
the summons to adventure in the form of a map, a riddle, a
fabulous tale, a magic object. Accompanied by an initiator, a
figure of demoniacal energy whom he simultaneously fears and
venerates, he undertakes a journey rich in sudden reversals,
difficulties, and temptations. He must overcome successive
trials and finally defeat a monster, or, more generally, confront
death itself. In the end he is reborn into a new life which is no
longer natural but artificial, a mature life and one of a delicately
vulnerable kind.

This plot is so well known[1] that I recall it to the reader's
mind only as a clarification of the use I ordinarily make of the
word *initiation,* employed in its least pretentious and most ha-
bitual sense. In this book a large number of initiatory journeys
are discussed: *Treasure Island, The Lost World, The Lord of the
Rings, The First Men in the Moon, The Star Rover,* and the two
journeys dealt with in this chapter. A mental review of the
works I have named suffices to prove that the pattern of initiation itself can serve vastly different aims and that the result
of the ritual can as well be the attainment of man's estate as
resignation, the enrichment of possibilities, or acceptance of
their finiteness. Both the journey of Gilgamesh and the quest
for the Grail are initiatory tales: the denouement of the first is
the inexorability of death, that of the second is immortality.
Epic wisdom always sees the journey as something significant;
for the storyteller, no one ever travels with impunity. But the
initiate's experiences vary from the most unmistakable triumph
of strength to the no less complete realization of weakness,
solitude, or annihilation. Initiation does not offer a lesson with
a single meaning; at its highest level, neither wisdom nor ignorance is alien to it. All these perspectives have already been
minutely studied by modern critics. I would like to emphasize
here some aspects of the actual experience of the journey in one
of its possible variants—the descent.

To descend is to plunge into that which sustains us, to plumb the foundations that lie beneath us. It is a dangerous mission, perhaps one leading to madness, for everything seems to indicate that the earth sustains us precisely insofar as it preserves its opacity, its stubborn resistance to our investigative gaze. To open it in any way is to put it out of action as a support; the investigation which uncovers it to our eyes takes it out from under our feet by that very act. Not only our physical stability but also our mental equilibrium, our reason itself, can falter in the course of this attempt. When we descend radically—that is, not when we descend a staircase, which is something raised, but when we descend to what is really below—we lose our firmest coordinates and have to invert our points of reference very oddly. What formerly upheld us now becomes something that covers us; what is closed surrounds us and opens before us, while what was formerly open acquires a faraway, opaque indeterminateness; to leap upward takes us closer to the rocks while falling brings us closer to the air. Our head no less than our feet needs solid foundations, and this exercise in geographical perversion can make it spin. Nonetheless, throughout the ages what lies beneath us has always been particularly tempting. The kingdom of the dead is there but also hidden treasures. The secret places of all things are there, which will permit us to control them better when we return to the surface. Whatever is deepest and most profound is there, which verbal intuition tells us is the most desirable. Everything decayed lies there but also everything that is forgotten, feared, all that must be concealed, that is, *buried*. There the deepest darkness awaits us— dead or alive, we will go there in the end, and to descend while we are still alive predisposes and prepares us for the last descent of all—and everything denied to the light of day. And there, lastly, down there, must be the center, for we cannot forget that we crawl about upon a sphere—and that center is not so much a geometrical equidistance as a point of spiritual power, the terrible divine umbilicus that contains the whole meaning of the world. One day we emerge from the nether, the dark, the enclosed places, from the earth; and on any night we will return to it. We descend in order to rise again, that is, to be reborn. This second birth endows us with renewed strength, an impeccable desire to live tempered by contact with hell, and a familiarity with fundamental things which causes the unavoidable to lose its horrible prestige.

We shall take our examples of the essential pilgrimage from Jules Verne. Curiously, though some descry in Verne the very paradigm of the initiatory novelist,[2] a critic as shrewd as Michel Foucault denies the initiatory nature of his tales, arguing that at the end of their heroes' journeys "nothing has changed, either on earth or in the depths of themselves." Perhaps here we would have to distinguish between the story of an initiation and an initiatory story: *Treasure Island* obviously belongs to the first category and Verne's novels to the second (with relative shades of difference which we will discuss). The story that narrates an initiation is the chronicle of the things that happen to a character in his progress toward initiatory enlightenment and maturity; in the initiatory story the reader is the initiate. Indeed, Verne's characters are usually purely external, eyes that see and hands that grasp, thermometers of temperature changes or bellows registering the absence of oxygen; their minimal inner selves are noted only in such primary phenomena as resistance to adventure (Axel in *Journey to the Center of the Earth*) or mystery: Captain Nemo has a secret, not a psychology. Following the initiation that undeniably takes place in Verne's novels, the characters display about as much change as the odometer of an automobile after the twenty-four-hour race at Le Mans: they register the distance covered, but otherwise are exactly the same as when they started out. But they have done their job of being the reader's eyes and ears during the initiatory process. Hence the documentary nature of so many of Verne's novels, his obsession with giving the reader reliable data about the circumstances of an adventure which concerns him more closely than the characters who are supposedly experiencing it, and who are really no more than the *sensorium dei* of the reader-god.

Reading Verne is like going up in an unballasted balloon, like riding astride a kite, like being pulled down into the abyss on a bottomless waterfall: and all this within the strictest and even the most prosaic matter-of-factness. It means dreaming, of course, but without having to give up calculation, reflection, and even plans. It means joining hands with delirium and placing myth at our service, only to reach the fullest and most irrefutable realism, to install ourselves irrevocably in the soberest ordinariness which surrounds us, accepted as imagination brought to life.

Let us say, in order to make ourselves a little clearer, that there are "hard" fantasies and "soft" fantasies. These last are rambling, cumulative, and unstructured, like their prototype, Lucian's *True History*; things that are portentous, unlikely, or conceivable only in the last resort by a generous stretch of the imagination succeed each other with the suspicious arbitrariness of a world where everything is possible except order. It is the realm not so much of the chaotic, which at least postulates an absent cosmos with which it contrasts, but of the amorphous. Since it is the only kind of fantasy conceivable by persons who lack imagination, and since it permits a certain harmful proclivity toward the allegorical, it has produced unreadable and pretentious jumbles like certain subproducts of German romanticism or a few French "rêveries". Let us, rather, remember the masterworks it has given us: *Alice in Wonderland*, Lord Dunsany's *A Dreamer's Tales*, H. P. Lovecraft's *The Dream-Quest of Unknown Kadath*.

"Hard" fantasy, on the other hand, prefers what Borges calls "the secret adventures of order" and abhors the gratuitous reversal of fortune as much as the juggling of inverisimilitude or the absurd. In this kind of fantasy surprise arises from careful plotting, not from incongruousness, and its most prodigious element is precisely the familiar gradations by which we approach the improbable. Certain rules of the game are laid down and respected, certainly broader rules than the usual ones but profoundly indebted to them, of which they are both extrapolation and counterpoint. In hard fantasy the most strictly regulated realities, such as ethics or science, can become the nucleus of the novel's plot. Let us recall with a thrill of gratitude *The Strange Case of Dr. Jekyll and Mr. Hyde*, the works of H. G. Wells and Olaf Stapledon, Arthur C. Clarke's *Rendezvous with Rama*, and others. Need we say that the works of Jules Verne are paradigms of the hard fantasy, that they not only aspire to attain the ephemeral triumph of perplexity but also the deepest and most permanent spells of prophecy, the initiatory ritual, and utopian freedom?

Apparently, Verne is anything but an *écrivain maudit*. His work enjoyed tremendous popularity almost from the beginning of his career, and his fame has remained intact, or even increased, to the present day, when his books have been published dozens of times in all civilized languages. But it has not only been the common reader who has supported him in this spontaneous and permanent vote of confidence; some of his most illustrious contemporaries had no hesitation in proclaiming his genius, with unaccustomed agreement: Tolstoy as well as Alfred Jarry, Kipling and Gorki as well as Paul Claudel, Raymond Roussel, and the surrealists.

Present-day French critics like Butor, Michel Foucault, Roland Barthes, and Claude Roy have "rediscovered"—the fashionable phrase—Jules Verne, burying the simple flow of his writing under mountains of Freudian interpretations, structural diagrams, or sociological digressions. It is an effort in which one is astonished as much by the writers' ingenuity as by their repetitiveness and superfluity; but I will not belabor the point, for maybe I am making the same mistakes on this page—in this book—and maybe I lack the gift of simplicity more than other writers do.

Verne was an unknown writer, they tell us, and the prestige he gained arose from a misunderstanding: he was confused with a "minor" author of the same name, taken for a simple writer of adventure novels or scientific prophecy, and his symbolic value, the mythical and political levels made possible by more "adult" readings of his work, was ignored. Miguel Salabert, his translator into Spanish, sharply accuses Verne's own readers of concealing these levels: "Readers of 'adventure books' are bad readers. Carried away by interest in the sudden change of circumstance, the story line, they unabashedly skip everything that they do not think essential. Descriptions and digressions bore youngsters."

Well, well, so readers of adventure books are bad readers

because they like good stories well told, without any false padding; good readers, on the other hand, enjoy putting up with the superfluous. So much for them, then, but where did Salabert get the idea that youngsters don't like descriptions and digressions? The youngster who is writing this read Salgari with other youngsters like himself, and it was not uncommon for us to rush off to verify in the pages of the encyclopedia one of the technical references to animals or trees that are scattered through his stories. No one is more meticulous than a child reader, my friend Salabert. In cases like Verne's, literary critics especially are made victims of their intrinsic limitations: *they* are the ones who have decided that writers of adventure or scientific prophecy are "minor," they are the ones who decree that adolescents enjoy only the picturesque or the unimportant, they are the ones who, in the nineteenth century, limited Verne's interest to his ability to foresee scientific advances and string together curious turns of plot. They are the ones who have always been mistaken about Verne; children, however, were right about him from the start. Now we must rescue Verne not only from his enthusiasts but from "serious" criticism's prejudices against "minor" literature. But even in the middle of this rescue operation, critics seize the opportunity to blame their own compulsions on those who have maintained a little freshness with respect to the stories' value, a freshness they have in large measure lost. Naturally mental retardation and childishness are not indispensable to make an adult interested in Verne: it is enough that he has not lost his capacity to enjoy reading. But this does not deny the fact that Jules Verne is indeed a writer of fantastic adventures and hence the possessor of a magnificent poetic and mythical spirit, like many other "minor" writers: Stevenson, Kipling, Wells, Salgari, Conan Doyle. Whether in the depths of the sea, in the clouds, in the impossible jungles of our nighttime terrors or on the moon, the voice of Jules Verne repeats his secret hymn, which sings persuasively of the many faces of courage, the miracles of reasoning power, and also—why not?—the paradoxical joys of resignation.

The first of the two Verne novels I have chosen to illustrate the downward journey is *A Journey to the Center of the Earth*, one of the most marvelous and unforgettable of the whole cycle. All of Verne is in it: the unusual scene, the tremendous enterprise, the timid and shrinking but resourceful adolescent, the energetic adult who performs the initiation, the untamable forces of the occult, the implicitly metaphysical meaning of risk and discovery. Professor Lidenbrock decides to give lessons in abysses to his nephew Axel: his plan is nothing less than to take him down to the very center of the earth. The adventure begins when they find an ancient manuscript written in unintelligible runic letters: it is the word of the Traveler, the Alchemist, which comes from far away, clothed in a ritual of concealment worthy of Poe. Axel does not want to answer this summons; his objections repeat those of a common sense that we might well call "superficial," since his chief argument is that everything that interests him in the world is on its surface and that he hasn't lost anything in that remote center. Lidenbrock, however, convinces him that to reach the center would best help him to possess the pleasures of the surface. What Paul Valéry said was true: "The deepest part of all is the skin"; the truth of this maxim lies in the fact that to regain the skin, one must first pass through the depths. Axel will take some time to learn this: he will take the whole novel, to be exact, for even when at the end of the journey he seems to be just as interested as Lidenbrock in reaching the center of the earth, this interest appears to be a sort of "rapture of the deep," more suicidal than regenerative. The center, after all, marks only half the journey: it is certain that the travelers have descended in order to come up, this time in a profound sense, to the surface.

We have spoken of *Treasure Island* as a reflection on audacity; we can undoubtedly think of *A Journey to the Center of the Earth* as an epic of effort. Few stories are so palpably toilsome, so humbly approving of effort and perseverance. It is made very clear that to descend is first of all a question of effort. Axel must undergo all the tests that effort has to face: hunger and thirst, exhaustion, vertigo, being alone in the dark, injuries, burns, disorientation, starting over, panic in the face of the

unknown, monsters of the lower regions, storms, the power
of lightning, rough waters, hurricane—and also obstructed
paths and blind alleys. Only his persistence in what he has
undertaken allows him to extract from weakness, in every case,
the necessary strength to pass the test successfully. In the chronicle of other exploits, what shines brightest is the heroes' skill
or courage; in this story the chief trait is obstinacy. Except for
the proofs of his passage which the long-dead Arne Saknussemm tried to make in order to mark the downward path, and
the positive indications in his manuscript, no special intelligent
initiative guides the descent of the travelers, who are fundamentally carried along by stubborn inertia. Rather than descending they seem to fall. And their ascent through the volcano
will be no less unplanned and will display the pneumatic au-
tomatism of the cork popping out of a champagne bottle. All
that is left for the travelers to do is put up with the confusion
of the different accidents of their journey, while they feel pressing above their heads those thousands of kilometers of rock
which, miraculously, do not decide to crush them. Perseverance
is second nature to Professor Lidenbrock, while the keenness
of his scientific knowledge is considerably less obvious. But in
this stressful descent wisdom is superfluous. All they need to
do is want, not to know or even be able to act.

As he descends, Axel finds more and more open space where
everything ought to be opaque, as we would think. Just as
modern atomic physics has shattered the solidity of matter,
making it identical to the near-emptiness of stellar space, so the
ever larger caverns encountered by Verne's explorers reproduce
the open expanse of the surface they had left behind. As Hermes
Trismegistus said, "What is above is equal to that which is
below." After descending many kilometers Axel reencounters
breeze and ocean, clouds and vegetation. Everything is the
same, but everything could not be more different. The lower
world is the past of the surface world, its ocean is what our
oceans have forgotten, its vegetation takes us back to the Jurassic
period or even earlier, its formidable beasts no longer harass
the earth's outer surface. A gigantic antediluvian shepherd
drives a flock of mastodons among giant ferns; the dust that

covers the ground comes from the calcareous remains of prehistoric mollusks. Just as memories of mute infancy pile up in
our unconscious, which is our lower depths, so the earth's past
is stratified and joined in its interior. The Herculean keeper of
mastodons is Utnapishtim, the Eternal Ancestor, whom Gilgamesh approached in his search for immortality. What seemed
hopelessly lost—the past—is only buried, has sunk, in order
to offer a solid foundation for our present. To descend is to go
backward. What sustains us is what precedes us. Axel will not
succeed in carrying the flower of immortality to the surface,
as Gilgamesh also was unable to do; the frozen, fundamental
shadow of Utnapishtim awakens his horror and postulates an
even more radical descent, of which he will no longer be capable. Really, only the young man has fulfilled the purpose of
the journey, for Professor Lidenbrock belongs to the abstract
scientific sphere of the dispute of forms, and the descent has
chiefly affected him as a verification or rejection of existing
theories. As for Hans, he fully belongs to the ferocious silence
of the primitive, as is revealed in the raft crossing under the
magical light of St. Elmo's fire. "Hans did not budge. His long
hair, blown forward by the hurricane over his motionless features, gave him an odd appearance, for the end of every hair
was tipped with little luminous plumes. This frightening mask
reminded me of the face of antediluvian man, the contemporary
of the ichthyosaurus and the megatherium."

Only Axel has truly descended, following the footsteps of
the alchemist Arne Saknussemm, but he does not succeed in
completing the journey of the perfect initiate. The center of the
world, which is perhaps ultimately made of fire, is closed to
him; the hasty violence of explosives he sets off will arouse the
bowels of the earth against him and result in his expulsion. In
fact this is the only initiative he takes during the whole trip,
and it causes the end of his initiation before he has completed
it. To descend is indeed a task for the tenacious man, not for
the merely resourceful.

Verne himself offers us another version of the voyage of
descent essentially different from the one we have just been
discussing. In this second version what opens beneath us is not

terrestrial solidity but the sea's unquiet skin. Here the descent is described as penetrating into another world that lies parallel to our own, not of diving into abysses that underlie and make possible the ground on which we move. *Twenty Thousand Leagues Under the Sea* promises by its very title a complete journey through this new territory. It is a parallel world, a qualitatively inverted reflection of the solid surface on which we live. This time the descent is not made simply to climb up again, as in the previous case, but to install oneself once and for all in the heart of everything that is different. The depths of the sea are literally for exiles. Those who choose it die to everything connected with their previous life. The crew of this wandering, ghostlike ship, the *Nautilus*, is made up exclusively of dead men. Its captain has lost his former name and rank and calls himself Nemo, Nobody, like Ulysses—but a Ulysses who does not perform this renunciation of his name as a subterfuge, the better to recover it later, but rather because this divesting himself of his name is meant to proclaim his permanent abandonment of the desire for Ithaca. To go down into the depths of the sea is a decisive step that does not admit compromise: it means turning toward absolute freedom. This is how Nemo puts it in his impassioned hymn to the sea:

The sea does not belong to despots! Up there, on the *surface*, men can still administer unjust laws, fight, tear one another to pieces, be carried away with terrestrial horrors. But thirty feet below the surface, their influence is quenched, their power vanishes. Ah, professor, why not live—*live* in the bosom of the waters! Here only will you find true independence! Here I recognize no masters! Here I am free.

But this freedom is won after a previous death at the price of power, a price that none of the three unwilling guests whom Nemo has plucked from the surface of the sea is willing to pay. On the other hand, that cold blue paradise is full of terrors, and to survive in it one must become a no less formidable threat. First taken to be a giant narwhal or some other kind of dangerous marine beast, the *Nautilus* indeed displays a wild animal's free will: its independence mingles with the exercise of ferocity. In no other way can it share the watery jungle with the hundred-handed horror of the giant squid, the man-eating cachalot—which is "nothing but mouth and teeth"—or the shark's swift, gloomy shadow.

Captain Nemo uses his marvelous submarine to carry out real challenges to natural forces. No matter how much he abhors terrestrial powers and their abuses, there is in him a large measure of the Faustian impulse that motivates the conquerors of empires or the inventors of volcanic war machines. Although the flag he plants in the frozen solitude of the Pole is black, something in his action reminds us more of Alexander's pride than Livingstone's humanitarianism. Nemo too, like his enemies the despots, understands independence as greater strength and greater resistance. This explains his tigerish wanderings, his defiance of the heavy, oppressive ice pack which traps him in a gelid coffin, his stubborn approach to the unendurable oven of the underwater volcano, and his defiance of the terrible pressures of the Sargasso Trench, where the *Nautilus* too succumbs to the temptation to descend farther and farther in search of "those primordial rocks never visited by the light of heaven; the lowest granite, which forms the very base of the earth; those deep grottoes scooped out of the rocky mass. . . ."

De Neuville's drawings successfully capture the haughty stance of this imperious libertarian, who was not content with shared power and sought the limitless kingdom of the sea for himself alone. His prisoners never succeeded in really penetrating his personality, which, we must recognize, was by no means easy. Aronnax's interests were too quiet and contemplative for him to feel entirely congenial with the pirate; Conseil's well-disciplined submissiveness might have pleased him even less. Ned Land, however, had a character that somewhat resembled Nemo's, but his perpetual rebellion did not awake in the captain the sympathy that might have been expected. After all, Land carried the earth in his soul, as indicated by his name itself; he was, moreover, extremely skeptical and dared to formulate objections against his very creator: "The common man believes in extraordinary comets crossing space, in the existence of antediluvian monsters in the heart of the earth, but astronomers and geologists don't believe in such fantasies."

Here is the voice of Verne himself, with his *Hector Servadac* and his *Journey to the Center of the Earth*. Axel at least undergoes a certain transformation, gradually becoming enthusiastic about the undertaking which his uncle and he have begun, but Nemo's three prisoners change nothing either in their relationship with him or in themselves in any fundamental way, though Aronnax duly marvels at the scientific aspects of the *Nautilus'* journey. In their best moments they behave like tourists and the rest of the time like prisoners avid to escape.

As we have said, however, the initiate that Verne's ritual of descent requires is neither young Axel nor the eminent Professor Aronnax but the reader himself. *Tua res agitur.* For you, bold reader, the hollow diamond, the echoing abyss down which the stone falls, bouncing from side to side, and the inner sea of our origins that awaits you in the center of the globe, if you dare to descend through the mouth of Sneffels which the shadow of Scartaris touches, before the calends of July. For you, reader who does not drown in a glass of water, the limitless turquoise sea teeming with creatures you have never seen or dreamed of, the shimmering ghost of Atlantis' sunken streets, the shining, blue-white torture of the ice—which Dante reserved for the lowest circle of Hell—contemplated from below, the spiral curse of the whirling maelstrom. Choose the way to the abyss that is best for you, the initials of the long-dead alchemist who preceded you in the descent, or the defiant sign of the great exile: the letters "A.S." scratched on the rock or the golden "N" that proudly marks the black flag.

# 4

## THE OUTLAWS' TRIUMPH

"Let this be a lesson to you, William Brown!" he said.
But William was no longer there.

Richmal Crompton, *William the Hero*

W HENEVER I FIND SOMEONE about my own age whose theoretical or ethical tastes resemble mine, someone, in short, who understands life as I do (that is, who doesn't understand it at all), I need not delve very far into his innermost and most congenial memories to find William Brown appearing in an aureole of glory. It is our common point of reference, the only necessary precedent, whose vibrant example we cannot do without. It is the lost link that unites us to a joy so far away that it now seems impossible. William Brown! No one, not Tarzan, not Sandokan, not even Sherlock Holmes, links us so closely together, explains us to each other so profoundly. The others can be reread, can be affectionately demythologized, can be returned to in one way or another, either through a pleasant pastiche or through cinematographic re-creation; but William needs no second reading. No effort whatever is required to keep the William-cult alive. We need only have made his acquaintance in time, when we were that incorruptible eleven years old which William stays forever, to keep him seated eternally on our soul's hearthrug, playing with his popgun or thoughtfully sucking an enormous licorice stick. It would be blasphemous to think of him simply as a literary success, which he undoubtedly is also; for William first of all is the hope itself that we will never lack the gumption to get out of a tight place. He is the name of the impetus that frees us from the impossible predicament, the trumpet blast that calls us back to the lists and invites us to victory. *Extra William nulla salus*: such is the motto of those of us who swear by the only triumphant anarchist known to history, the undisputed captain of the outlaws.

I believe that part of William's success was based on the deplorable appearance of the middle-aged lady, a friend of my mother's, who gave me the first of his books. One naturally had the deepest and most justified contempt for that dull monstrosity, so dear to our elders, known as a "children's book," a libel that used to combine in a hateful mixture, along with a plot fit to disgust the worst-endowed connoisseur of reading, some moral maxim derived from the most egregious idiocy or

Richmal Crompton's "William" books have delighted generations of European children, but have never been published in the United States.

sadism, and illustrations whose artistic merit consisted in a hor-
rid assemblage of violent colors and unnecessarily detailed
drawing. That was exactly the kind of book one expected from
the lady in question, and when on one of my first ten birthdays
she put the little package in my hands, saying, "You'll love it,
dear, it's such a *nice* book for you," the immediate and most
logical reaction was to toss the suspicious gift into the garbage.
But fortunately I did not do so. I tore off the paper and there
was William, no more and no less.

At first the look of him confirmed my worst fears: good
heavens, they were stories about a *little boy!* I must make it clear
that the most despicable thing about "children's books" was
the children who invariably figured in them: either obedient to
the point of slavishness or naughty to the point of crime, lucky
or unlucky without having done anything to deserve either fate,
suffering from the exemplary wrath of a set of commandments
they had decided to illustrate at their own expense, given to the
most vacuous occupations and the least attractive games—in
a word, utterly stupid. Ah, how often we laughed about it
later, for having been able to think that William belonged to
that feeble group! And how we enjoyed the treatment that the
great outlaw reserved for that monster's spawn, bearing a vague
resemblance to the usual protagonists of children's books, who
had the misfortune to cross his path! The surprise afforded us
by reading William multiplied our enthusiasm for him from the
very first. He was the sun coming up in the west when we
needed it most, the improbable turning out in our favor.

What an exquisitely happy mistake, what secret irony of the
gods, could have caused that tiresome, perfumed lady, whose
taste in all areas of the spirit could not possibly have been worse,
to present me with that extraordinary marvel? It was as if a
policeman were to hand out picklocks, or a vampire volunteer
to give blood. But then we learned, precisely by reading William's adventures, that the world is full of eccentric ladies behind
whose alarming appearance good fortune lurks, waiting for us
to let it approach. Hail, unworthy old lady, fairy godmother—
we know it now—who one day brought us William, as if to
tell us that the most precious things always come this way,

without warning, and that we are scarcely able to believe that they have really arrived! Come back whenever you like, but don't fail to come! One day, after the sweets that cloy and the too-familiar caress, in that hour when we anticipate nothing but boredom, may the marvel present itself again and the miracle come to life, just as when, on that faraway occasion, a despairingly accepted "children's book" became the shining legend of William Brown!

It is astonishing how easily one slipped into the circumstances of William's life, which after all were entirely different from those of a Spanish boy of my generation. The lush green world of a small English town, more like a village than a city, with its cottages, its vicar and his wife, its confusion of pennies, guineas, and half crowns, its greenhouses, its absurd charity teas, all the constant references to a foreign history and culture, the old-fashioned air of the otherwise excellent drawings by Thomas Henry—each of these things and all of them put together should have placed us at a vast distance from William's adventures, making them only a little less exotic than if they had taken place in the Congo or Indonesia. Which would have no importance if William were a literary character, for whom it was possible or even desirable to do something unexpected or exotic; but it could be fatal to the playmate by definition, the great director of games, to whom we resorted every afternoon so that he could lead our group and whose chief virtue, the fundamental merit that justified his differentness, was that he was, without a doubt, just like one of us. Precisely because he was one of us could we admire his splendid peculiarity; the fact that he shared our tastes, our duties, and our limitations allowed us to enjoy his triumphs as if they were our own. Everything that set him apart from our everyday existence weakened him, tended to make him into a phenomenon belonging to distant places. Mowgli was marvelous, but one had to remember that he was an Indian and had been raised with wolves; Ivanhoe was unforgettable, but not everyone has the good fortune to be born a knight at the court that had been usurped from Richard the Lionhearted. One could dream about these characters or even imitate them, but always at a certain distance: William's adventures were made to be fully *lived*, with nothing interposed between him and us. With William there were no distances, nothing separated us from the model; it was an unemphatic gospel without any supernatural interventions to make identification with the savior difficult.

François Mauriac, asked at the end of his life who he would have liked to be, once said, "Moi-même, mais réussi." William was myself, but completely successful, me at my very best, at the tip-top of my energy and good fortune. If this had not been true everything would have stayed mere literature. William was not a more or less unattainable ideal, but the joyous fulfillment of my best possibilities. His first and perhaps greatest exploit was to wipe out all the differences between his environment and our own, that is, to preserve them as concrete peculiarities of the adventure but not as exotic features that would dilute the verisimilitude of their contours or characteristics. And so we all sought our old hut in the house where we were spending the summer or attempted unsuccessfully to distill that fabulous mead, licorice water. It was not a question of "playing at being William," as we played at being Tarzan or Sitting Bull; it was a question of playing *with* William and, in homage to the usual additions to his exploits (unnecessary additions, for our own would have been just as good as his, but recognizable by affinity), we drank to the health of William and his outlaws in licorice-tinged water.

When I reread some of the "William" books before writing these pages, I observed with some astonishment that they are composed of short independent adventures. Though it may seem surprising, I had not remembered that. I keep the great outlaw's saga in my memory as a seamless continuity, in which not only the chapters but even the different books disappear and only the different days of my life with William remain, like the mornings and afternoons of our friendship. Adult readers of Richmal Crompton are able to point out one or another of William's adventures to me as particularly successful, while they find others insipid or boring. I suppose that as readers they can't be asked for more than that. But such opinions are valueless compared with the magic memory of friendship with

William, an experience one has when one reads him at the right age; then what one really wants is to be with him, even though it means doing nothing, and then one even enjoys the less exciting or even disappointing passages, as on those Thursday afternoons when we friends would try three or four games and none of them turned out well, but we were left with a feeling of grateful warmth toward our friends just because they were there and we had tried the games together. William did not teach us to ask for things but to wait alertly, with patience and in the confident expectation of good fortune. He only needed to be there for the adventure to have the greatest probabilities of success; he was a sort of lightning rod of good luck, the great supplier of surprises, the undisputed master of the seized opportunity. Was? It is hard for me to speak of William in the present tense. It must be because I am afraid of infecting him with my present wretchedness, with the abject submission of the grownup. Peter Pan complex, William Brown syndrome? Idiots can find plenty of nasty names for the burning, stabbing pain of our rebellion against time, to justify as "normal" the decline of body and soul, the pact made with resignation and the compromise with fear, the renunciation of willingness to take risks and commitment to brotherhood, the surrender to the abstract prestige of what can't be helped, the betrayal of generosity—the guilty relegation of William to oblivion.

In Carlos Castaneda's excellent book on Don Juan—perhaps we should speak of Don Juan's books on Castaneda (however that may be, they form the most profound and original nucleus of writing published in the United States for many years)—the "impeccable warrior" is presented as a fundamental concept, one which Don Juan frequently applies to himself and Don Genaro. This concept, easier to describe than to define (as happens with all ideas which not only refer to relationships between different terms but also require the presence of an example of action to be understood), refers to the unfailing strength of the man who succeeds in gathering all his energies to attain an objective that eludes him, combining intelligent respect and even fear for the laws of the given with a perfectly aware consciousness and full confidence in himself at the moment of action. Well, if there has ever been an impeccable warrior in this world, that warrior is William Brown. The only difference between him and Castaneda's characters is that they reach their privileged status by means of a demanding asceticism and a self-discipline directed by knowledge, while William is *born* an impeccable warrior, or at least he became one as the result of an unclassifiable experience, as privately and exclusively satisfying as masturbation. The warrior ethic that rules William is as invigorating as—or more invigorating than—the virtue of strength which, according to Plato, must restrain the irascible temper of the Ideal City's guardians. He is brave, and even rash on occasion, but he has a coldblooded realization of his own limitations and always tries not to allow his boldness to carry him from mere diversion to disaster; he enjoys the element in violence that leads to physical detumescence and quickness in avoiding injury but never its cruel aspect—magnanimity toward the vanquished is the only glory that the victor certainly does not owe to luck. William is impetuous, but he loves the calculated ins and outs of strategy; he seeks the joy of discovery and the challenge of risk rather than booty; he prefers spiritual booty— the grateful smile of a blonde, blue-eyed little girl, the prideful admiration of his gang—over objects to be collected and counted. He seeks these last for others rather than for himself. After all, he always has the reward of being William. He can put up with a good deal but is not ascetic; he is imaginative but logically so; he is romantic up to the point where this disease is still compatible with irony, pragmatism, and a taste for cream buns.

According to the legend, the goddess Athene so dearly loved the warrior Tydeus, father of Diomedes the horse-tamer, that she made up her mind to grant him immortality. She waited until he had fallen on the field of battle and then rushed toward him to give him a drink of the ambrosia that would rescue him from death forever; but she saw with horror and revulsion that the ferocious warrior, carried away by the inhuman passion of combat, was using his last strength to try to devour the still-warm brain that was oozing through the cracks in a fallen enemy's skull. Indignant, Athene poured out the ambrosia on the ground and let Tydeus die. I cannot imagine that William would have given her an excuse for such a tantrum; he comes from that shining line of captains for whom a fallen enemy ceases to be of any interest, even as food. Obviously, cannibalism is the sort of idea that often arouses real enthusiasm in William, although not as a diet or revenge but as an adventure. Though Robert Graves once reminded us that Homeric heroes knew nothing of sweets and concentrated their preferences on large roasts of meat, our impeccable warrior feels a decided liking for desserts; he is a greedy Achilles, a Hector inclined toward filled chocolates.

And also, perhaps rather than anything else, he is Ulysses, he of the winged and subtle word, he who invents a thousand stories and is capable, to save himself, of appearing as a criminal or a beggar, he who negotiates everything, the king of agreement and deception, the best advocate of his own cause. William's oratorical resources would have left the wily king of Ithaca pale with envy. The versatility of his verbal talent is literally inexhaustible: he is as good at ferocious sarcasm as at self-enhancing flattery, no less brilliant in the bitter hour of protest against injustice than in the hymn that praises his own triumph or extols the excellences of a person he loves. What is particularly notable is his skill in saying exactly the right thing in that first remark that begins a relationship. The ordinary citizen in such a situation is apt to get lost in conventional formulas that reveal nothing or in distrustful allusions, but William goes right to the heart of things, opening fire with "Can you stand on your hands? I can." Or he states succinctly, "I'm a pirate." Through such a procedure the least promising relationship usually becomes interesting at once.

No less admirable is his gift for carrying on a conversation whose meaning and context he knows absolutely nothing about, letting the other person talk and answering in monosyllables surrounded by adverbs, to thin out their precise meaning: "Yes, quite well . . . ," "Not always," "Yes, yes indeed," and so on. This skill is complemented by a diabolical facility for picking up any shred of affirmation brought forward by his interlocutor (likely to be an old lady who takes him for her

long-lost nephew, a vicar who thinks he is an orphan suffering
from amnesia, or even a young woman whom he has convinced
that he is a youthful agent of Scotland Yard with the job of
shadowing a Russian prince). When the hypnotized creature
suggests to William, under the mistaken impression of acting
out of free will, something like "I'm *sure* that you are . . ." or
"I wouldn't be surprised if you had to . . . ," William is offered
the necessary foothold for his transfiguration to continue. Now,
it absolutely cannot be deduced from this that William is a
deceiver; he is, simply, conscious of his many-facetedness and
consequently uses it on his own behalf. He is less mythomaniac
than mythological, less an actor than a visionary. Two essential
qualities guarantee the adventurous character of each of his
mutations. In the first place, he always respects to the end the
internal logic of the character he has assumed; that is, if he has
decided to be an orphan or a Red Indian, he will use in his
battle for victory the resources appropriate to these character-
izations. In the second place, each of his impersonations faithfully preserves the ethical traits of the eternal William; he is not
simply a gangster or a bear but William the gangster or William
the bear. And so he is as faithful to the multiple part of himself
as to the single part. During these transmutations he bases himself chiefly on the word to convince others and the deed to
convince himself, that is, to enjoy himself. He knows that a
suitable speech will change a child and some feathers into a
space animal, or a bottle of licorice water into rum, but he also
needs to *do* something about what has been changed by the
magic word, so that what has simply been described may be
carried to the highest efficacy in play. The contradiction of the
situation usually breaks forth on this delicate point, as Hegel
foresaw, and the illusion dissolves in a crisis as a result of which
William can begin to play at something else.

In William's speech, two forces coexist that make bad part-
ners but in this case lend each other strength: fantasy and logic.
William is a careful and well-organized dreamer, whose restless
imagination extracts a good part of its power from the strict
organization of his form of speech. There is nothing soft about
him, nothing weakly gratuitous. The constant invention of real-

ity is the daydream of the person who has no energies to confront the harshness of the given, but it is the quickest path to adventure for the person who decides to take risks. It is a question of setting one's imagination in motion. Sleep for William is not a refuge to evade practical activity; rather, it is precisely in praxis that the dreaming capacity finds its manifestation and exercise. William's logical strength surprises us by the straightforwardness of his arguments. The secret weakness of persuasive speech is to elevate its inexorable success to a logical demand, by this means condemning to external control both the person who uses it and the one who receives it. But in William logic is not a dictate of control but an impulse of freedom. It is a coherence that springs from passion, not a limitation imposed by necessity. Hence, for example, William decides that there *must* be pygmies in England because there are forests, which is where pygmies live; he is offered the argument that if this were true someone would have found them, to which he replies that this is not necessarily so, given their small size and skill in hiding. Then he is told that he can't find them either, to which he immediately ripostes that he is exactly the right person to find them, given the fact that his size and skill in hiding are identical to those of the pygmies. But will it not be dangerous to run across these savages? "No," says William, "because I can be savage too, if they are." Result: the outlaws, headed by their dauntless captain, start off immediately and, without too much effort, find pygmies in the heart of England. The fact is that pygmies are not an anthropological category, nor a particular geographical area, nor even a certain kind of pig, as William at first thought, but they are decidedly a summons to emotion, a possibility of adventure, the final objective of William Brown's impeccable logic.

William's life is lived in two areas which are almost diametrically opposed from every point of view: on the one hand his family and on the other the outlaws. The list of radical contrasts could be very long: closed versus open, monotonous versus varied, what one is told to do versus what one chooses to do, the expected versus the unexpected, the ridiculous versus the sublime, the arbitrary versus the fully meaningful, duty

versus pleasure. Generally speaking, *penury* in all its meanings—
emotional poverty, careful spending, limitation of expectations—compared with *abundance*, considered in a no less general
way—treasures of passion, extravagance, infinitude of possibilities. But this contrast is too rigid and could give rise to a
simplistic kind of Manichaeanism according to which the family
would be a compendium of all evils compared with the outlaws'
spotless perfection. From this to trivializing William, making
him a rebel against family tyranny, requires only a step, which
perhaps a certain "progressive" taste would permit. Contempt
for one's parents, however, is a wretched kind of vocation
which William's impassioned generosity does not countenance.
William adores his family with all the intensity of which his
vibrant spirit is capable; he adores it without ceasing to struggle
against its limitations or to slacken his active protest against
what he is told to do. Unwittingly, the whole family is under
William's protection, which is often a source of concern to both
sides. The threats that weigh on the stoical Mr. Brown's fi-
nances or the health of his languid and not very intelligent wife,
Ethel's embarrassing or irresistible suitors, and Robert's artistic,
political, or mundane activities, without counting the unnum-
bered problems or seeming problems (in William's eyes) which
afflict the picturesque uncles, cousins, great-aunts, etc., of the
clan—this whole struggling universe contains innumerable trib-
ulations which William takes on himself with absolute seriousness and faces with a businesslike efficiency usually thought of
as too expeditious by those who benefit from it. William is not
the dissolving chord but the tonic note of this family world,
and it is not his fault if it often happens that such a well-worn
environment does not survive the radical treatments he admin-
isters. Our hero's spontaneity is, in any case, above all suspicion. William is very well aware of his roots and is grateful to
them—his strength does not admit the resentment of the base-
born, who always find those responsible for their ills too close
at hand—but he is not inclined to permit them to immobilize
or mutilate him. He is too loyal to confine himself to mere
obedience, loves his family too much to accept being like them.

The outlaws are freedom in company. They partake a good

deal of the nature of a band of nomadic hunters, and somewhat of a crew of buccaneers. William is the chief for the same reasons that Akela became captain of the wolf pack in which Mowgli grew up: he always runs ahead, jumps higher than anyone else, and has a better nose for the clues that lead to the prey. William's enormous prestige among his followers and the gang's deeply felt confidence in him are, however, accompanied by the ever-present possibility of protest from below, which the slightest setback produces; his followers' grunts of protest whenever they get bored or when something turns out badly are a permanent spur that preserves William from any threat of somnolence or routine. The outlaws must be won over daily; thus they require a constant effort on their captain's part, in exchange for which they offer him their unconditional loyalty and a personal devotion that goes beyond what is demanded by simple duty. William's orders are never flat, unexplained ultimatums, but form part of that storytelling in action which is always the outlaws' game. William holds the general key of the story that underlies the game, and distributes roles or proposes moves in a reasoned relationship with it. These games have no element of silent diversion or mechanical pastime but are the poetic fruit of a militant imagination. The outlaws are undeniable precursors of every other form of poetry in action, and William is their born chief because he is the one best capable of telling them the story of what they are doing. This correlation that they experience between action as discourse and discourse as action is a defining constant at every moment of William's saga. Who has outlawed the outlaws? Precisely the power which perpetuates a life split between the family's soothing affection and the free camaraderie of friends, between the power of imagination and the demands of logic, between the availability of theory and the need for praxis, between mercy and courage, between that which preserves and that which intensifies. This split is presented as inevitable, and leads to a wounding choice: one must either give in or run away from home, one cannot simultaneously be a pirate and the child of a family. But the outlaws refuse to make the choice; because they are still young enough, they choose everything at once and flout the split that outlaws them. Their memorable lesson is none other than this: everything that perpetuates division is false. The conformist in bedroom slippers as well as the ferocious rebel who burns his boats behind him collaborate equally in an order which the dilemma's inevitability merely strengthens. *You need not give up anything, you need not renounce anything*: the path that is defined by exclusions and renunciations leads to death. Is this a glorification of fleeting adolescent indeterminateness? But to say that is to take for granted that growing up means realizing the need for the necessary! It was precisely a question of doubting this kind of wisdom, no matter how many venerable parchments attest to its prestige. William, Ginger, Douglas, Henry, entrenched in their old hut, prepare for an expedition; adventures will not be lacking, for luck does not forsake those who have denied necessity and have been outlawed for it.

Shall I reveal at last the secret of William's victorious career? Here it is. In every case, at every moment, William is able to adopt the hero's point of view. The legend that he never stops telling, to his friends and to himself, is recounted from the highest point, from the triumphal summit, where everything acquires vigorous meaning, including—chiefly—defeat. His enemies, the wretched Hubert Lanes and Herbert Franks who circulate in the world, play the game with all the advantages offered by money acquired without merit or cleverness and the unconditional support of the status quo. But they lack what is most important, what is indispensable for victory, the state of mind that makes a hero immortal. In their intrigues they do not succeed in adopting the hero's point of view. It is a perspective fraught with danger, which constantly borders on despair, which must always be ready to wager everything on a single throw, must not look constantly over its shoulder; but it is the only viewpoint that can aspire to real reward, to the prize that does not come from outside but forms part of that reward, *is* the reward, if the description serves. William never hesitates over anything essential; that is his magic.

I would like to be able to tell you something about that old lady dressed in black, Richmal Crompton, the English schoolmistress who was able to adopt the hero's viewpoint so perfectly in order to tell us William's saga, but the fact is that I know nothing about her. I do view as highly significant the fact that it was a woman who so successfully brought to life that virile dream of a perfect, predatory adolescence which William personifies. After all, the brotherhood of free and irresponsible men is only conceivable from the matriarchal standpoint. How many libertarian paths are closed off by the masculine concept of rationalism, a concept based on the systematic forgetting of the essential! But, after having made so much literature about William, I hardly need to begin writing emergency anthropology. The hero's viewpoint—there is the secret. Without it, one can only be an honest person, a man of the world, a well-intentioned reformer of society; but with it one can be all that and anything else too, pirate, redskin, bear, conquistador, detective, dragon, rebel, outlaw, misunderstood, a genius, just like William Brown.

# 5

# THE LAND OF
# DRAGONS

Beyond was the long sweep of the woods, and in the center, shimmering vaguely through the gloom, was the great lake, the mother of strange monsters. Even as we looked a high whickering cry, the call of some weird animal, rang clear out of the darkness.

Sir Arthur Conan Doyle, *The Lost World*

I THINK THAT not much has been written on the enormous importance of dinosaurs. In addition to their obvious biological interest dinosaurs have an enviable mythical importance and an epistemological resonance of primary significance. In the biological sphere others better informed than I could speak at length about the proliferation of the reptiles with sonorous names who covered land, sea, and even the sky of the remote Jurassic period, becoming all by themselves a whole, complete zoology. It is their mythical and epistemological aspects that I would like to emphasize here. The dinosaur's legendary qual-

ity consists in responding satisfactorily to an inner longing of the romantic soul which Tolkien once expressed in these terms: "I desired dragons with a profound desire." Borges remarked in his study on Germanic literatures that the dragon infects with puerility all the stories in which it appears; that is true in some measure, but it neither denies nor lessens our profound desire for dragons, a desire deeper than any longing for literary maturity.

In its scaly bulk the dragon unites ferocity and unhappiness, sorcery and tellurian forces, the last obstacle that prevents the conquest of the treasure and the miserable resignation of a creature who sees himself tied for centuries to a hoard of wealth he can enjoy only as a guardian. The frightful product of the earth's entrails, his breath is fire, his wings invite flight, and something in his silhouette and certain of his appearances seem to confirm that he is a marine animal; moreover, a bath in his blood confers invulnerability, and his sperm—jade—is a guarantee of immortality. He is all that is dark and incorruptible, the necessity of death or the key to everlasting life. The dragon has no substitutes in the imagery of our archetypes. How can we not be grateful to paleontology for its generous evocation of terrible, flesh-and-bone lizards—for us, unfortunately, now nothing but bone—which sate our desire for dragons in a rationalistic way? Obviously they are not as satisfactory in their mythical function as the authentic dragons of legend, but they compensate, with the scientific stamp of approval that guarantees their existence, for some of their most obvious structural deficiencies; less ethical and nostalgic than those which inhabit fairy tales, the dragons of paleontology are much richer in strange shapes and in the suggestion of a blind and devastating savagery.

Naturally, what we know about the behavior of these reptiles is mere scientific conjecture, that is, rationalist legends, probably influenced by the story of Beowulf or of St. George: in a certain sense dinosaurs are the terrifying progeny that sprang from the eggs laid in men's imaginations by the mythical dragons. And so we return to the epistemological value of these thunder-lizards. Has it occurred to anyone that dinosaurs are the first great romantic hypothesis which triumphs over the positive, antimarvelous common sense of modern science? Indeed, when scientific attention began to be paid to the first fossils—in studies by persons as famous as Leonardo da Vinci, Francastoro, or Georgius Agricola—there was a strong tendency to think of them as simple stones with fantastic shapes and not as the petrified remains of extremely ancient animals.

Lay rationalism refused to believe what Leonardo himself considered convincing proof of the reality of a universal flood, when remains of marine animals were found on land and far from where they could reasonably be supposed to have been carried by natural forces. The positivists of the period spoke of a *vis plastica* of nature, which amused itself by imitating mineral and vegetable forms in rocks. As late as the eighteenth century Voltaire jokes about fossils found in Germany, which for him are no more than simple pebbles manipulated by the priests to prove their fraudulent claims. After all, was not this opinion the most logical and "scientific" one? Let us forget for a moment what has been taught us as an irrefutable victory of modern knowledge. Does it not seem much more likely, more rational, more like real science, to suppose that the apparent bones and apparent traces encased in rocks are the product of erosion or mechanical foldings of the earth's crust, rather than to proclaim the astonishing theory that they are the remains of monstrously large dragons and elephants who made tangled, nightmare jungles shake with their titanic battles, millions of years before the first man was born? And yet it was the astounding hypothesis that was revealed as the most convincing one. The dinosaurs proclaimed the supremacy of imagination as opposed to the mutilating self-censorship of rationalist common sense, for which "mediocre" means "probable," and every discovery that disappoints man's secret legendary desires is immediately considered to be eighty percent confirmed before any further proof is forthcoming. Cruel tyrannosaurs, ponderous stegosaurs, diabolical pterodactyls like medieval kites, your impossible shadows emerge from the museums to come to the rescue of old tales, to appease in some measure our desire for dragons, to correct the positivist scientists' mania for distrusting everything astonishing and rejecting everything unusual or thrilling.

One of the most amusing satires on modern scientists, their academic quarrels and their reductionist but vigorous view of reality, is also one of the best adventure novels that this century has produced. It is Sir Arthur Conan Doyle's *The Lost World*, a novel in which he creates Professor Challenger and which is among the best-told yarns of this extraordinary storyteller. Nowadays the plot seems trite to us owing to the innumerable imitations it has had to suffer (among the best of these are the series on the island of Caprona and on Pellucidar, both the result of Edgar Rice Burroughs' remarkable inventiveness). It can be summarized as follows: Professor Challenger, while traveling through South America, discovers traces of prehistoric life in the jungles of the Amazon. He returns to London and prepares an expedition to prove his theories. These explorers find an inaccessible tableland in the heart of the jungle, inhabited by antediluvian beasts and native races at the dawn of human development. After a great many dangers they return to London with surprising proofs of their discovery. Conan Doyle succeeds in telling the whole adventure by always placing the reader at exactly the right spot to enjoy it most, so that each scene acquires a sort of joyous magical intensity. *The Lost World* is a novel that one reads in a permanently gleeful state of mind, appropriate to the night before a holiday or the dreamy excitement of an early dawn on the day we are going to undertake a long-desired journey. It is a book written with great good humor, in which the author infects his readers with the pleasure afforded him by the writing of every page.

The characters of the two scientist members of the expedition, Challenger and his rival Summerlee, are amusingly raked over the coals. Both are stubborn, incapable of any pleasure that does not derive from classifying things or beating the other to a discovery, but despite everything slaves to a kind of fanaticism which at times could almost be mistaken for greatness. Challenger in particular is a walking metaphor of nineteenth-

century scientific savagery, the privileged exponent of what
Giambattista Vico called "the barbarism of thought." His physical aspect is so similar to that of a caveman that the chief of
the prehominid tribe which takes the explorers prisoner spares
his life because he thinks he is a fellow caveman. But much
more barbarous than his outside is his inside, where his internal
physiognomy is that of a genuine Attila the Hun, despoiler of
myths, anticlerical, antimagical, demolisher of the fog of hesitation in the face of the incomprehensible and belief in the
marvelous that characterizes the most human side of all that is
human. Challenger is the essence of the Faustian concept which
knows no other form of approach to the real than manipulative
use of whatever exists. All his classifications, measurements,
and searches for the efficient cause of every phenomenon have
no other objective than *control*; knowledge is knowing how to
manipulate. This manipulation is clothed in the legitimizing
cover of the useful, but ultimately Challenger's true aspiration
is to proudly satisfy his pure desire to dominate, as is seen in the
surprising short story "When the World Screamed," which tells
how Challenger discovers that our planet is an enormous animal, a sort of colossal sea urchin, and devises a way to drive
an enormous drill into one of its sensitive spots, producing a
bloodcurdling scream from the maltreated earth. But, difficult
and vain as he is, it cannot be denied that Professor Challenger
has real class, a prodigious capacity to expand the limits of the
probable on the basis of a handful of firm facts, a vibrant theoretical imagination, and energetic determination which recoils
from nothing when the time comes to carry out his plans. In
the ethical sphere, however, and this is Conan Doyle's irony,
his character is surprisingly old-fashioned. Challenger is a mixture of supreme theoretical sophistication and maximum rude-
ness of behavior, observable even in his most positive aspects,
such as his childish, irritating sense of humor or his fierce concept of personal dignity, appropriate to a Tiglath-pileser III but
not to a British academician. For good and for ill, a form of
barbarism was reborn with the positivist, enterprising, scientifically optimistic spirit of the nineteenth century, a form of
barbarism that tramples on the web of subtleties, distances, and

respects which are the most refined product of civilization, but which are also, perhaps, the paralyzing beginning of decadence.

*The Lost World* begins and ends with two tumultuous academic sessions that possess an absolutely priceless narrative liveliness and comic tone. Malone, the journalist who wants to perform some act of derring-do in order to win an indifferent sweetheart, is present at the first of them and offers to accompany Challenger as a volunteer on his ambitious quest for the prehistoric plateau. His journey will be an initiatory experience of a deeply ironic kind, for when he returns after having overcome terrible dangers, worthy now of his lady's heart, he finds her married to an insignificant little man who has never had any adventures beyond the insurance policies and file cabinets that go with his job as a solicitor's clerk. This final disappointment is the real proof that completes Malone's initiation. At the first academic meeting, two other explorers join the expedition: Professor Summerlee, a colleague and rival of Challenger's who decides to travel with him in order to check his unlikely claims, and Lord John Roxton, a hunter, world traveler, and soldier of fortune, who merely wants to add another spectacular foray to his already extraordinary list of exploits. The latter, with his nerves of steel and his unyielding bellicosity, will become in some sense Malone's mythical model, that perfect fighter into whom his initiatory journey must eventually change him. In the end, with his prospective marriage broken off, Malone will return with him to the plateau that time forgot.

The general session of the Zoological Institute with which the novel concludes, however, is the book's truly unforgettable scene. The chapter is told in the form of a newspaper article and begins with interruptions by unruly students and skeptical professors, much like those which had so skillfully added interest to the academic meeting where the journey had been decided on. But the tension gradually grows greater. The explorers have lost most of their scientific documents, all their photographs, and the most significant part of their paleontological collections. The audience has to take their incredible declarations on trust, with no proof but their simple word. Naturally skeptics appear who are unwilling to do so, and who try to deflate the Assembly's popular success. Then Challenger has a large packing case brought in, the only thing that the expedition's members have preserved from their astounding journey. He opens it and leans over it, snapping his fingers and coaxingly calling upon its occupant; an instant later the detestable figure of a live pterodactyl appears perched on the side of the case. Alarmed by the tremendous hubbub to which its presence in the room gives rise, it begins to fly about among the audience and finally escapes through an open window. The brisk, vigorous tone with which the scene is described, the image of the antediluvian creature terrorizing a convention of paleontologists, the accumulation of cleverly placed, amusing details—all this stimulates to the highest degree the pure pleasure of reading the passage, a pleasure that owes no debt to anything, a pleasure subservient to nothing and directed toward nothing. Ever since I read those perfect pages, I have never again attended a lecture or scientific debate without harboring the hope that a real dragon might suddenly appear in the room and disturb the rarefied air of the foreseeable with the extraordinary flapping of its membranous wings.

In some hidden corner of the Amazon, inaccessible as a forbidden love, rises Maple White Land, the plateau that time forgot, explored for the first and last time by Professor Challenger's little expedition, the legendary and marvelous land of dragons. The blood-red light of a pitiless sun beats down on giant ferns and enormous blocks of lava; in the Central Lake the snakelike head of a plesiosaur breaks the surface, while hundreds of pterodactyls crowd around a blue-clay volcanic tube, full of diamonds no one wants. The tribe of ape-men spends the daylight hours digging traps along the paths used by the great mammals to reach a water hole, and pointed stakes rear up in the depths of camouflaged pits. At nightfall the antediluvian thicket is transfixed by a burst of roars, spine-chilling in their avidity. The great carnivorous dinosaurs, as well as the wholly improbable sabre-toothed tiger, have gone hunting; in the indifferent moonlight there are attacks and struggles such as the human eye was never meant to endure. In their precarious caves high in the rocky cliff, the prehominids tremble before the shadowy jungle's furious lash, and people their helplessness with the alternately terrible and benevolent shapes of their primitive gods. Everything that is familiar to us today has not even begun.

I would not like to be the primordial creature who lurks and dreams in his cave but the traveler who comes from the future to exemplify fully that quotation from Karl Kraus: "The end is the beginning." In some sense that is who I am when I dream of dragons and dinosaurs, of a living darkness purified of the obsessive presence of victorious men. No doubt it is only an adolescent fancy. I remember myself very clearly, in bed, at thirteen, my eyes moist with strange yearnings and passions, entrenched in the darkness. On the one hand I felt that it was impossible that anyone could be so perfectly miserable; on the other, I could not shake off the inner conviction that there could be no one in the world happier than I. Then, maybe without ceasing to cry, I would reconstruct step by step the path that led to the lost world. I would timidly join the Challenger expedition and entrust myself to Lord John Roxton's unerring aim. I would go with Malone on the night path of terrors and monsters that leads to the Central Lake. I would hear behind me the dreadful panting of the tyrannosaur ready to spring. I would flee, running with terrified joy through the shadows of the land of dragons. Long before I was overtaken by my tyrannous pursuer, I would fall asleep dreamlessly, in the peace of the Lord.

# 6

# THE PIRATE
# OF MOMPRACEM

"Sandokan," said Yáñez, "I think you are very worried."
"Yes," replied the Tiger of Malaysia, "I do not hide the fact from you, my dear friend."
"Do you fear some encounter?"
"I am sure that I am being either followed or preceded, and a seaman is not easily deceived."

Emilio Salgari, The King of the Sea

I THINK OF MYSELF as the lucky discoverer of a jealously guarded identity—despite the publicity given to all the data in the case—and one essential to the proper understanding of adventure in modern letters. I fearlessly concentrate my discovery on one lapidary phrase: Sandokan was Captain Nemo's father. The consequences of this unexpected revelation make the lamest imagination soar, but even at the risk of numbing my reader's just-awakened curiosity, and by virtue of my literary *droit de seigneur* as its discoverer, I will venture—or better still in this case, I will adventure—some initial lucubrations about this relationship, as undeniable as it is important.

I point out in the first place the most obvious resemblances between the two characters. Natives of some small island in the Indian Ocean, of aristocratic and even princely origin, both were forced by a massacre in their families, and the loss of their small respective kingdoms, to engage in piracy with an implacable hatred toward the English Crown, one upon the sea and the other beneath its surface. I will be told that these resemblances are not sufficient to certify the paternity I have postulated, but there is a great deal more. In the first place their physical resemblance, for Nemo takes after his father in all essential details: the identical stature, tall without being extraordinarily tall; the identical proud, robust bearing; the same thick black beard; the same eyes, sparkling with uncontrollable brightness under heavy brows; the same very dark complexion—as racially both would naturally have—the same dominating air and identical elastic, catlike step.

Even more surprising are the similarities between their characters. Both are introverts, given to melancholy and morbid meditation, though full of courage and able to perform the boldest actions without a moment's hesitation; both are austere and even cruel, but endowed with great generosity and a strange, deep kind of compassion for the weak and persecuted. The one no less than the other values freedom and independence above all else, and both demand from those around them absolute fidelity and unquestioning friendship, to which they re-

Emilio Salgari's tales of adventure continue to have an eager following in Europe, but they have never been translated into English.

spond in even larger measure. Both have an extremely high opinion of themselves and limitless pride, which is sometimes revealed in signs of excessive, almost neurotic, susceptibility. Both love the sea because it is broad and free. Are not these details sufficient for someone who, like me, has that "genealogical sense of smell" noted by Nietzsche? And on the other hand, the dates correspond too. The declaration of war on England signed by Sandokan in the full flush of his manhood on board the *King of the Sea* is dated 1868, the twenty-fourth of May to be more exact, while Nemo's apogee must be placed in the first two decades of this century. I believe that all this is more than sufficient to enable me to state, without the shadow of a doubt, that under the Latin pseudonym of the *Nautilus'* captain was concealed the sonorous name of the terrible pirate of Mompracem.

Now that this has been established, the history of rebellion demands that we measure the differences separating the two men, and the change in the spirit of defiance that we can glimpse by observing those differences. Sandokan is a much more luminous, more *solar* rebel than Nemo. There is a certain romantic ingenuousness in him which makes him vibrate with that optimism-in-retrospect known as nostalgia, even in the heart of his gravest misfortunes. For Sandokan is frequently defeated; every three chapters or so we find him with ships sunk and the crew decimated, proclaiming his permanent farewell to his faithful little Malaysian tigers or even to himself, as at the end of *The Pirate's Wife* when, as he sees that his red flag has been carried away by a cannon shot, he exclaims, "Farewell, piracy! Farewell, Tiger of Malaysia!" But immediately we see him reorganizing his forces and getting ready to make a bold strike against the Rajah of Sarawak or even the English viceroy himself.

Between Sandokan and Nemo lies all the distance that separates nostalgia from despair. For the pirate of Mompracem, while there's life there's hope. Even revenge is a conserving principle, for the first thing that it requires is to protect oneself as much as is compatible with courage. Nemo not only denies all hope, but denies life itself. For him, his *Nautilus* is a submersible and destructive coffin whose men have given up light, life, and joy from the very moment they took ship. In this accursed submarine the instinct of preservation itself is something that must be combated, for a man whose soul is dead does not care whether he dies today or tomorrow. Nemo's final appearance in *The Mysterious Island*, transformed into a dying, semidivine protector, also confirms this image. His loss of aggressiveness gives the impression of being chiefly due to physical decline, not to a final concession to optimism which would reconcile him with some aspects of the order of things in the world. Despite the threatening tone of some of his actions, Sandokan rebels in search of personal self-determination, and the enhancement of his person by high-sounding titles—"Tiger of Malaysia"—or impressive declarations of war on his enemies—"I, Sandokan, on board *King of the Sea*, declare war on England and all her allies . . ."—is never a simple accessory that can be dispensed with in his warlike undertakings. Captain Nemo, on the other hand, has carried his infinite pride to the point of self-annihilation. His name is Nobody, like Ulysses', but he has not adopted this pseudonym as a measure of prudence or the key to some ruse but as an appropriate realization of a negative megalomania. In the whole Indian Ocean there is no one who can defeat Sandokan, master of the sea; but only limitless nothingness can be compared with Nemo's funereal greatness.

The pirate of Mompracem's exploits are characterized by relatively utilitarian aims, which are absolutely alien to the inventor of the *Nautilus*. Like Nemo, Sandokan seeks vengeance, but he also seeks riches, swift ships, and above all Mariana's love. This detail is the essential point of difference between Sandokan and Nemo; the Tiger of Malaysia is deeply in love and allows himself to dream from time to time of the safe and beautiful island where he will live till the end of his days with his adored "Pearl of Labuan," surrounded by his faithful Malays. On one occasion, seemingly almost frightened of himself, he confesses to Yáñez, "Listen! I love that woman so madly that if she were to appear to me now and ask me to give up my nationality and become English, I, the Tiger of Malaysia, who have sworn eternal hatred to that race, would do it without hesitation! I feel an unextinguishable love that runs through my veins, that lacerates my flesh!"

For Nemo there is no human consideration that would make him desist from his somber mission or cause him to abjure his principles. His hatred is no longer exclusively centered on the English and their allies, though he continues to prefer them at the hour of annihilation, but he has logically extended it to the rest of the human race. He is a dead man who hates the institutions and customs of the living, their vices, their cruelties, their stupidities; but above all he hates their antlike proliferation and, secretly, the insatiable loves which sustain that proliferation. It is not a mere play on words to say that Sandokan is more superficial and Nemo deeper, because we must point out that really life is only a thin film covering the earth's outer skin and that in the rarefied depths of the abyss it is the possibility of life itself, not merely disdain for it, which disappears. The destructive judgment launched by Nemo from the depths of his lucidity against everything human is made inevitable by the extraordinary honesty of his descent down the precipice of hatred. In the depths where nothing lives, Nemo's lament resounds; many fathoms above him, Sandokan searches for Mariana and fights for her ferociously. Nemo's only grand passion, apart from his desire for annihilating revenge, is scientific knowledge. But science reinforces rather than mitigates his yearning for death. It does not function like that love which—Sandokan realizes this—eventually makes a person renounce all action not directly inspired by the affirmation of life. For the lovesick pirate of Mompracem, even his hatred for the English ends by being secondary; the only real thing is Mariana, name of his heart's desire, and even the national flag on which he had concentrated his hate is in the end forgotten, like a convention that interferes with what is really important. Thus love corrects everything that turns aside from life; science, on the other hand, permits all errors except theoretical ones.

Despite the sympathy he feels for him in the scientific field, Nemo does not succeed in becoming friendly with Aronnax, for the latter's desire to live separates them. The scientific wisdom of the *Nautilus*' captain has become, moreover, devastatingly disinterested, and he carries out his risky experiments—crossing the polar icecap under water, descending to unheard-of depths, rashly approaching underwater volcanoes—with the indifferent glance of the transcendental subject Kant postulated for authentic scientific knowledge. His wisdom makes Nemo especially invulnerable; compared with him, Sandokan is always in a precarious position.

The Tiger of Malaysia's contact with science is purely external. He uses but does not understand it, and in his heart of hearts perhaps he does not approve of it. The exploit of the *King of the Sea* is very revealing in this respect. Sandokan captures a formidable American battleship, *King of the Sea*, a real, unsinkable colossus of its period. Compared with the junks and native vessels that the pirate has commanded until then, it is an immense qualitative leap. Fascinated by this machine of fire and iron, he declares war on England, on the Rajah of Sarawak, and all their allies. In a sense, he sees in the battleship's powerful structure an adequate materialization of his defiant will. After several invariably victorious adventures against lesser adversaries, Sandokan finally runs up against a British squadron that has been sent to look for him. It is made up of four battleships, each of them as large and powerful as the *King of the Sea*. Then Sandokan learns of the infinite repeatability of every scientific product, which for that very reason can never be adequately adjusted to man's indomitable individuality. Strength does not reside in the *King of the Sea*, a machine that can be duplicated or perfected at any time, but in being Sandokan. Science still offers him a last hope in the shape of an eccentric American inventor whose secret weapon sinks one of the enemy ships with great ease; but immediately afterward a cannonade finishes him off and destroys his instruments, which nobody in the pirate ship, of course, would have known how to use. Salgari is emphasizing in this episode the radical incompatibility between his hero's specific courage and the kind of triumph offered by merely technical superiority. That was not victory for Sandokan. One of the finest moments in the saga of the pirate of Mompracem is when he is willing to go down with his great ship, defeated by a superior enemy but knowing that in the most essential element he is unconquered.

The *Nautilus*, by contrast, is a direct prolongation of its inventor; it is less a ship than a prosthesis. Nemo's genius and his extraordinary knowledge have allowed him to create a ship in his own image and likeness; each of its exploits can be attributed directly to its fabulous captain. But this is due to the fact that Nemo is a very different kind of man from his father, Sandokan, though he is a man who has the same familiarity with machines and the scientific-technical mind as Sandokan with his scimitar or with courage. The superscientist succeeds in individualizing himself, at least quantitatively and cumulatively, by means of his brain. However, to preserve his superiority, the scientific genius has to keep on refining his inventive capacity endlessly, to avoid the duplication that will standardize his originality. Time runs against him; in fifty years, the *Nautilus* and the *King of the Sea* have become vulnerable museum pieces, while Sandokan's lovelorn *terribilità* and Nemo's fathomless despair keep their mythical value intact.

From father to son, rebellion has become harder to achieve. There are scarcely any islands left on the face of the globe wherein to seek refuge and repair ships that have suffered in battle, and the indomitable spirit must hide in the deepest and most desolate part of the bitter ocean. From that vantage point Nemo will try to confront the knowledge of power with power itself, inventing new and disconcerting weapons that will replace the clean courage of yore. But at the hour of decisive confrontation the two banners of the rebellious soul will fly together: the red flag of the pirate of Mompracem with its tiger-head device and the black flag stamped with a gold "N"—the initial of "nobody" and "nothing"—of the solitary submarine wanderer.

Sandokan is the adventurer chemically pure, despite the vengeful and even political trappings he seeks for his exploits. His is undoubtedly the most fully realized figure that the desires of the heart—the gods who dictate stories to men—presented to Emilio Salgari, the unforgettable poet of action and of the exotic. I know that I have enjoyed this Italian author more than

Verne or Walter Scott, who are both undeniably superior to him. No doubt the special charm of his literary faults, with which his work is happily plagued, contributed to my liking for his works. His taste for encyclopedic information about the most extraordinary peculiarities of the flora, fauna, and customs of the lands where his novels take place frequently causes him to abstract a whole chapter from the logical course of the story to introduce a tree or an orangutan. The somewhat confused rhythm with which he tells some adventures, with curious jumps in time and space, gives the magical impression of living them in a dream. The immediate giveaways in the plots and their transparency make them seem like the strange result of destiny (for instance, in *King of the Sea* one chapter is inexplicably entitled "Suyodhana's Son"; this makes us suspect that an officer in the Anglo-Indian navy who appears in the chapter must be the offspring of the Thugs' terrible chief, which is revealed as true at the end of the novel with all the earmarks of a tremendous dramatic flourish.) His jerkily laconic dialogues are so picturesque that they produce effects worthy of the best Zen. And so on.

Salgari was sufficiently talented to lack talent, something that is not as easy as it seems. To measure the breadth of his inventiveness, we need only take a look at the sources from which he drew documentation for his stories. The saga of Sandokan is based solely on Louis Rousselet's *L'Inde des radjahs*, for atmosphere; *Il costume antico e moderno*, by Giulio Ferrari, for the decor; an Italian version of *Le Tour du Monde*, the wonderful geographical magazine, and vague inspirations taken from Mayne Reid. But Salgari knows how to preserve the best parts of the books he uses in the very smell of his novels. For example, his characters always move through landscapes filled with the crowded charm of engravings by Riou or Thérond, the marvelous illustrators of *Le Tour du Monde*, which bear little resemblance to the color photographs of the *National Geographic*, to use a more up-to-date comparison. His inventiveness is essentially evocative; just as a paleontologist reconstructs the prehistoric animal from a single bone, Salgari conjures up a whole India full of epic possibilities with no other assistance than the fuzzy illustration in an encyclopedia or ten lines from some dubious traveler's tale.

A recent series of films on Italian television has brought new popularity to the figure of Sandokan among people who had forgotten him or even knew nothing about him. It seems that the scriptwriters of the series place great emphasis on the pirate of Mompracem's characteristics as a third-world rebel and make him the leader of the fight against imperialism. The most beautiful, the most profoundly useful thing about heroes is that they always return, clothed in the particular desires for liberation which each historical period nurtures. The truth is that Sandokan was most certainly not a "democratic" protagonist, that his authoritarianism verged on the despotic, and that strictly personal considerations spurred him much more strongly than a few nationalist ideals which were fundamentally quite alien to him. And yet, beyond the mediocre political maneuverings of the professionals of domesticated revolution, who try to reduce everything to a single game which they have already betrayed, Sandokan is clearly a subversive symbol. The man who wants to fully live adventure, liberty, and love always feels the colonial yoke on his neck, even if he lives in the capital of empire. The tigers of Mompracem rise up against that power which controls everything through its rationalized violence and whose codified rancor knows nothing of the noble explosion of fury. That power has kidnapped all the Marianas of the world. Sandokan tells us—and it is a lesson so subversive that it smashes into fragments the very idea of politics as the infamous art of perfecting control—that everyone who does not want to die a slave must be the protagonist of his own passion. It is a terrible message that he brings us, and formulated abstractly, as a pure watchword, it can even resound with equivocal accents of barbarism in the new era. Between us and the joyous individual adventure which takes pleasure in its very risks, the shadow of the sinister swastika will fall for a long time yet.

How difficult it is to be conscious of this and yet not renounce adventure! Storytelling is precisely what helps us to do it, showing us by example that the hero's strength is ethical—the memory of the primordially important and of generosity, faith in life—against which no ethic of force can finally prevail. And even if it should prevail, the hero would not cease thereby to be a hero—and he would still win in everything essential! In this respect, Sandokan's attitude is luminous, sunny. But let us not burden it with austere transcendentalism, whose seriousness always loses sight of the fact that a joyous lightness is the most important thing. We must embark, without giving it any more thought. We must force our way into the jungle, which offers terrible wonders at every step and ignorance of which may cause the death of the careless traveler. We are threatened by the power of Sir James Brooke, the rajah who exterminates pirates; and in some hidden part of the thicket crouches the temple of bloody Kali, from which the formidable Suyodhana sends out his Thug stranglers against us. But begone, fear! At our side is the quiet, wily Yáñez de Gomera, our brother-in-arms; Tremal-Naik and the giant Sambigliong cover our rear, along with all the lesser Malayan tigers who are ready to die with a smile on their lips for their Tiger. Reward? The only reward is the adventure itself, but the adventure is Mariana.

"No, my brave one!" she said, "I ask nothing but happiness at your side! Take me far away, to any island; but where I can love you without danger or risk!"

"Yes! If you wish, I will take you to a faraway island, covered with flowers, where you will never hear the name of your island of Labuan or I mine of Mompracem; to an enchanted isle in the great ocean where the terrible pirate, who has left torrents of blood behind him, and the lovely 'Pearl of Labuan' can live together in love. Do you want to come, Mariana?"

"Yes! But hear me: a danger threatens you, perhaps a betrayal, which at this very moment is being planned against you."

"I know it!" exclaimed Sandokan. "I foresee betrayal, I feel it coming; but I do not fear it!"

# 7

## DWELLERS IN
## THE STARS

Yet across the gulf of space, minds that are to our minds as ours
are to those of the beasts that perish, intellects vast and cool and
unsympathetic, regarded this earth with envious eyes, and
slowly and surely drew their plans against us.

H. G. Wells, *The War of the Worlds*

THERE CAN BE NO DOUBT that the planets of our solar system, and even those that revolve around inconceivably distant stars, are inhabited. They are inhabited by our ghosts, our aspirations, and our fears. They are governed by insatiable magnifications of earthly tyrants or monstrously swollen reflections of the soulless bureaucracies we have to endure, while mercilessly exact and precise scientists—that is, still more *sci-*

AMAZING STORIES

Stories by H.G. WELLS

*entific* than ordinary scientists—forge obsessively efficient machines. There, insects grow until they reach human size and rear up on their hind legs, just as has been happening forever in our nightmares, while language is abolished in favor of the immediate telepathic communication we have wished for so often and so foolishly. The human element everywhere, even in the far corners of the universe; we cannot bear to let anything escape our activity, our observation, our manias. The leprosy of conscious life spreads like an infection from planet to planet, leaps from sun to sun, at least on a hallucinatory level.

When he imagines dwellers in other worlds, it seems that man would modestly resign himself to losing his central position as the navel of the cosmos. But no. In an ecstasy of supreme arrogance, which establishes once and for all his total incapacity for moderation, he mentally conquers galaxies, scatters images of himself about the stars, frantic because he cannot yet go and sully them in person. Each apparent retreat of anthropocentricity is really a subtle reinforcement of the desire for control of the cosmos—at least theoretical control—which is the essence of that ineradicable vice. Indeed, Galileo's system is more anthropocentric than Ptolemy's but less so than Newton's or Einstein's. Earth is too small to satisfy human cosmic vanity, which decentralizes intelligence in increasingly sophisticated systems in order to make the whole universe gravitate around a type of thought that occupies not only the center but also the periphery and every corner of all that exists, permeating with its laws the very last particle of stellar dust that floats in the tiniest portion of ether.

No matter how extravagant a form can be imagined for the beings of other planets, they are monsters who think, and that makes them our brothers, because the definition of man is exactly that. Centipede-men, men with tentacles and suction cups, water-men, fire-men, pyramid-men or cylinder-men, what does it matter, they are all men in the first and last instance, beings who think, who unfailingly place themselves at a distance from themselves and from what surrounds them, who feel hatred or ambition, who pity each other, who feel sorrow, who organize and rebel against organization. The scene of the human comedy expands, becomes complicated, becomes exotic; costumes grow more elaborate, the setting more sophisticated; the plot stays monotonously the same. Man has poured his own anxieties onto the stars and then fearfully scans the infinite silence of space; the invaders whom his fears await are coming to return the intrusive visit his imagination paid when it disturbed the perpetual irrelevance of the void.

The new race which will descend from the heavens, as Vergil sang, brings us no other novelty than an exacerbation of our tendencies, an accentuation of our actions to the point of ridiculousness or atrocity. We want to contaminate the universe with speculative thought, to extend the anomaly of consciousness to the farthest nebulae, to aggravate on other planets the complications we endure on this one. We want to save ourselves, of course, and we can travel only in one direction; once we have known spirit we cannot go backward, cannot blot out its traces, fall back into a mineral existence. We must flee forward, must endow all forms and all worlds with intelligence, to make thought burst forth up there and return to the paradise of harmony by way of an intensification of diversity, through a judicious emphasis on conflict. We have been extraterrestrials ever since we succeeded in looking at Earth from outside, from afar; the monster who plans our world's invasion in another world is the hope of that radical difference which the spirit's ennui cannot be resigned to relinquishing. Only from intergalactic space, now, can the barbarians come whose invading thrust is the answer to our most secret desires. Or, better still, only on other, even more decadent and confused planets than our own could we behave like barbarians and warm our icy blood by looting outworn civilizations, in comparison with which even our jaded species would become an ideal of vitality.

The two paradigms of our relationship with extraterrestrial beings were stated by Herbert George Wells in his novels *The War of the Worlds* and *The First Men in the Moon*. I obtain two obvious advantages in referring to these two classics rather than tracing the subject through the erudite meanderings of science fiction. Both are directly related to the subjective whim and the sloth—or lack of bibliographical material—that rule these pages, as I warned the reader at the outset. In the first place, I have not enjoyed any later recreation of the subject as much as Wells' splendid novels, which I consider to be not only the successful beginning of a genre but also one of the highest points in that genre; in the second place, confining ourselves to two stories as clear-cut and direct as these will strip our encounter with the aliens of tiresome casuistry or endless ramifications. I cannot resign myself, however, to omitting mention, though merely as a list of titles remembered by chance, of other stories of this kind which I have enjoyed hugely.

The first of the two models—the *War of the Worlds* paradigm— tells of the invasion of our planet by beings from outer space and the earthmen's more or less successful struggle to keep them from conquering their world. Its line in science fiction is so long that it is hard to imagine that new changes could be rung on the subject, though I have no doubt that they exist. I recall with great enthusiasm *The Day of the Triffids* and *The Kraken Wakes,* both by John Wyndham; *The Whisperer in Darkness*, by Lovecraft; Zenna Henderson's benevolent, biblical invaders in her *Stories of the People* and *Food to All Flesh*, compared with the astounding visit of Arthur C. Clarke's *Childhood's End*, Robert Heinlein's *The Puppet Masters*, Frederic Brown's *The Mind Thing*, and Theodore Sturgeon's *Killdozer*.

The second model—whose paradigm is *The First Men in the Moon*—relates a space voyage to another planet (I have just read the last few words and remembered Borges' tongue-in-cheek observation, "after all, every journey is a space journey . . .") and the clash of the earthling invaders with the beings who live there. It has produced no fewer a number of variants than the previous type, of which those I am about to list have caused me special joy: first of all, Ray Bradbury's *Martian Chronicles,* which I still find magnificent; the adventures, on Mars and Venus, of the indefatigable gladiators imagined by Edgar Rice Burroughs; Stanislaus Lem's splendid novel *The Invincible*, or *Le Signe du chien* by Jean Hougron, who as far as I know has no other contact with science fiction; a wonderful story by Lord Dunsany entitled *Our Distant Cousins*, and an uncharacteristic story by Lovecraft in which the inhabitants of Venus shut an earthling up in an invisible labyrinth (*In the Walls of Eryx*).

But I shall not go on with this enumeration, which is as arbitrary as it is limited by memory's whim. I only meant to refer, by way of an always pleasant recalling of titles I have enjoyed, to the apparently infinite number of variants permitted by both these paradigms, a variety that will necessarily be excluded from the treatment of them I am about to undertake. Besides, an over-detailed discussion of the two conventionally established models would have to include the always tiresome frontier quarrel of the cases which swing between one and the other without wholly belonging to either. In which paradigm shall we include A. E. Van Vogt's tremendous novel, rather childishly known in Spain as *Los monstruos del espacio*—the original title is *The Voyage of the Space Beagle*, a charming homage offered to the fascinating memory of Darwin's voyage—in which a gigantic terrestrial space ship, a real microcosm, is repeatedly attacked by horrifying stellar creatures? According to whether we concentrate on the *Space Beagle*'s journey or on its aspect as an invaded mini-Earth, it can be placed either in the first or the second model. An opposite but by no means conflicting case is that of Arthur C. Clarke's masterwork, *Rendezvous with Rama*, which relates the exploration by an expedition from Earth of a gigantic artificial asteroid that enters the solar system, inside which the expedition finds a whole surprising world made by an unknown race. Here it is an alien miniplanet which invades the solar system controlled by the human race and is in its turn invaded by a commando from Earth. I imagine that a more solidly based erudition than my own could multiply endlessly the typical and atypical examples of both paradigms. I shall limit myself to these few indications, which demonstrate both the subject's complexity and the shortcomings of the treatment I have chosen to give it; let us go on without further ado to a discussion of the two H. G. Wells stories.

*The War of the Worlds* is a sensational piece of reporting. With well-calculated convincingness, in an eyewitness style to which the war reporting of the early twentieth century had accustomed

his readers, H. G. Wells takes the best possible advantage of
the kind of fabulous news story his tale presents. This aspect,
that of an incredible up-to-the-minute reportage of Martian
invasion, was also skillfully exploited by Howard Koch, the
writer of the radio script based on Wells' novel, whose broad-
cast in 1938, directed by Orson Welles, caused a shudder of fear
in a North America which did not yet clearly foresee the war
of worlds in which it would soon be engaged.

In some sense the Manichaeanism to which war reporting has
accustomed us is faithfully reflected in Wells' story. The Martians are repulsive, greedy, blindly destructive monsters who
feed like vampires on human blood. They have no likable or
even positive characteristics, unless their technological advance-
ment is to be included in this latter category. In the anatomical
description offered of them, we are told of a radical reduction
of the visceral system in favor of an enormous development of
the brain. The Martians literally have no entrails, they are all
head. A similar vision of extraterrestrials is offered in the presentation of the Grand Lunar in *The First Men in the Moon.*
According to Wells, our interplanetary neighbors are essentially
calculators; what these monsters personify is the hypertrophy
of pure reason, an emphasis on the implacable trait of intelligence. The immediate simplicity of the feeling of aversion
aroused by the absolutely different and hostile makes the
reader's reaction all the more positive because of his sympathy
with the terrified flight of the novel's protagonist. Few stories
have the quality of being lived from within like this one by
Wells. What he does is to show us, with absolutely convincing
realism, an everyday scene in devastation, but one which, in
moments of the most fantastic anomaly, falls back into ordinariness through some masterfully presented detail. Wells succeeds in bringing all this destruction very close to us, and we
unhesitatingly accept the besieged earthlings' reactions as plausible, just like those we would fear, or hope to find, in a violent
swirl of public disaster. Even the Martians eventually become
familiar to us, after the initial moment of fundamental strangeness has passed; little by little we become accustomed to terror,
recognize its characteristics, resignedly work out dodges to

palliate its effects, and this accustoming ourselves to horror ends by being more horrible then the horror itself.

The protagonist flees through an England that has suddenly been fragmented by the attack from space, among vividly depicted scenes of collective panic and desperate attempts to believe that the authorities will eventually restore normal conditions. Anything, the passage of a train apparently unaware of the chaos or a regiment of soldiers in disciplined formation, is frantically hailed as a sign that order is being restored, that the change in people's lives has been brought under control. Sometimes a picture of heroic resistance appears whose hopelessness makes it all the more telling, but it is not brought down to the level of the pointless action of the suicide trying for a medal.

During my adolescence I used to feel shivers of martial emotion at the moment when the ironclad *Thunder Child* turns to face the invaders. The scene is described with a peerless sense of rhythm. Along with a group of fugitives, the narrator's brother boards a paddle steamer from the Thames, while hundreds of small vessels crowded with people try to reach the open sea to flee to the Continent. At that moment the giant Martian tripods appear, whose Heat-Ray has already earned a reputation as invincible, and take to the water in great leaps, as if they wished to cut off the terrified vessels' retreat. Suddenly "a vast iron bulk like the blade of a plough tearing through the water, tossing it on either side in huge waves of foam . . . and rushing landward . . . and from that twin funnels projected and spat a smoking blast shot with fire. It was the torpedo-ram, *Thunder Child*, steaming headlong, coming to the rescue of the threatened shipping." The ironclad's cannons manage to account for two Martians, the first that have fallen since the attack on Earth began. The Heat-Ray splits the valiant ship in two, and it goes down without ceasing to fire from bow and stern and after having succeeded in assisting the flight of the endangered ships.

At this point in the novel the Martians' superiority has become so overwhelming that the action of the warship that dared to defend the honor of the British Navy and the fugitives' lives is welcomed as a real breath of hope. But soon all dreams of victory vanish, and people must acknowledge that the conquest of Earth has been consummated. The survivors live by hiding underground in the ruined cities, working out vague plans for revenge or loudly repenting their sins which have brought this punishment upon them, directly and literally from the heavens. Strange red weeds brought by the invaders grow lushly in the streets of London, choking the ruins of the buildings that had formerly been the pride of a whole civilization. Like tormented beasts, men experience a brutalization, with no future and no initiatives to be taken. This is the way Wells describes one episode of that period:

"One night last week," he said, "some fools got the electric light in order, and there was all Regent's Street and the Circus ablaze, crowded with painted and ragged drunkards, men and women, dancing and shouting till dawn. A man who was there told me. And as the day came they became aware of a fighting-machine standing near by the Langham and looking down at them. Heaven knows how long he had been there. It must have given some of them a nasty turn. He came down the road towards them, and picked up nearly a hundred too drunk or frightened to run away."

Reduced to the status of flocks to provide meat for the Martians, man lives out his end as a conquering and dominant species. Without the unexpected help of the humble microbes of Earth's atmosphere, there would have been no possible liberation for him. In any case, it is certain that he was no longer able to look at the stars with the untroubled complacency with which he had observed them for centuries before the Invasion.

The style of *The First Men in the Moon* is noticeably different from that of the novel we have just been discussing. The magical naturalism of *The War of the Worlds* changes to a Victorian humor whose tones become darker and darker, ending with the cruel irony of the story's final pages. The idea of a trip to the moon was already established in literature when Wells wrote his novel, for Verne had dealt with it not long before in two of his most popular tales. But Verne was wholly preoccupied with the journey itself, its technical difficulties and most important incidents; he did not dare let his characters set foot on the moon's surface, possibly because he did not know how to solve convincingly the problem of their return. Wells, however, dispatches all the scientific obstacles that obsessed Verne with the sardonic invention of a marvelous substance, Cavorite, which is resistant to the force of gravity; with a sphere covered with suitably placed Cavorite plates, it is the easiest thing imaginable to travel to and fro in space, thus eliminating all the annoying explanations about fuel, propulsion, friction, and other technical trifles and leaving the whole object of the voyage reduced to its essential core: exploration of the moon and the encounter with the Selenites. Verne was possessed by the militant fantasy of electricity and the internal-combustion engine, whose inexhaustible possibilities he praises with imagination and enthusiasm; but Wells is more interested in the social tale, in the stellar utopia, and the surprises that he reserves for his reader come from the confrontation of cultures and forms of organizing conscious life rather than in scientific prowess.

The two earthmen who are to be the first men in the moon form a truly extraordinary pair. Cavor, the inventor of Cavorite, is a modest interplanetary Edison, ingenuously positivistic and ambitious only for the fame offered by the monthly bulletins of the scientific academies, who goes along with Bedford, an untalented writer obsessed by the sort of business deals that make a man rich in a hurry. The moon's inhabitants are intelligent insects who live in complicated galleries under the planet's surface; at night they take out huge, stupid, tame flocks to feed on pastures that grow instantaneously. They possess a rigid social stratification and are also distinguished by the same cold overdevelopment of the intellect that characterized the Martians who invaded Earth. Cavor and Bedord are taken prisoner; soon their greater muscular strength and the agility afforded by the moon's low gravity make them highly uncontrollable by the Selenites. These ultraorganized people, who are peaceful to the point of boredom, among whom no kind of violent conflict exists, are deeply perturbed by the appearance of the two earthlings, made extremely dangerous by confusion and a feeling of persecution. Bedford heedlessly knocks down a number of Selenites and manages to flee in the Cavorite sphere, leaving behind on the moon poor Cavor, who is less adaptable to crime and also too much interested in the prospect of new discoveries promised by the adventure to concentrate all his energies on flight. Once safely back on Earth, Bedford carelessly loses the sphere and with it the possibility of going back to search for Cavor. An Italian amateur radio operator receives a message from our satellite, sent by the marooned inventor. According to his own account, Cavor was brought into the presence of the Grand Lunar, the supreme authority over the whole planet; above a rudimentary body is a gigantic brain which servants constantly spray with a cooling liquid to prevent congestion. The ruler interrogates Cavor about the earthlings' habits and customs. He is appalled by the absence of a single authority and concerned about the (to him) incomprehensible institution of war. He astutely makes certain that Cavor is the only person who possesses the undesirable secret of the substance that permits travel through space. By eliminating him they will eliminate the danger that bloody barbarians could upset the moon's equilibrium with their quarrels and rapacity. Wells gives the traitor who abandoned his friend on the moon a vivid dream, with "a blue-lit disheveled Cavor struggling in the grip of a great multitude of those insect Selenites, struggling ever more desperately and hopelessly, as they swarm upon him, shouting, expostulating, perhaps even at last fighting, and being forced backward step by step out of all speech or sign of his fellows, forevermore into the Unknown— into the dark, into that silence that has no end."

The most elementary lesson that can be drawn from both novels is this: encounter with the inhabitants of other planets can only bring us conflict, either because our own passions are so uncontrollable or because of the total absence of such passions among the extraterrestrials. The most serious thing about this conflict is that it allows for no valid mediation, possesses none of the usual insulators that normally soften confrontations between men. The enemy is always the other, the nonhuman, something in relation to which the rules that regulate violence within the human community do not apply. "Thou shalt not kill," we say, and we mean "Thou shalt not kill any man, any fellow-human, any of your own kind, who exhaust the limits of what is human." But the being who comes from outside, from outside the humanizing circle of the community, can and must be killed, just as when some man through a serious fault falls from humanity and becomes alienated from it. Most human groups have begun by calling themselves "the Men" or "the People"; the noun *human* has a profoundly exclusive and condemnatory origin. But little by little men have succeeded in recognizing certain resemblances to their enemies, have thrown bridges over the irreducible abyss of their hostility. The enemy may have certain gods on whose faith he will swear when making agreements, he may be familiar with honor and mercy, and this will reduce the destructiveness of any conflict with him by a certain number of degrees. There are limits that the warrior may not exceed in his contempt for the vanquished foe; he cannot treat him as something absolutely *alien* to himself. Athene was especially fond of Tydeus, a blameless warrior, and had decided in her heart to make him immortal; the goddess waited until he was lying mortally wounded on the battlefield, and then descended toward him bringing the ambrosia that would make him immortal; but she found that Tydeus, in a last paroxysm of uncontrollable ferocity, was clawing open with his dying hands the split skull of a dead enemy to gnaw on his brains like a wild beast. Athene spilled the ambrosia on the ground and let Tydeus die because he had not respected the fallen warrior's human dignity.

Gradually there came to be established a few minimal resemblances among the different groups of men who claimed for themselves exclusive possession of what is defined as human, and because of those resemblances the hostile confrontation that embittered their conflicts was softened. Biological similarities, identical needs and fears, certain common interests respected by the logic of both groups aid in this approximation to each other. But suppose that man confronts enemies who have no resemblance to him either in physiology or habitat or any tastes or needs? What mediation can alleviate the destructiveness of their confrontation?

Extraterrestrials offer us the specter of unlimited violence, of the final abolition of everything that protects the life of individuals and restricts the victor's right to looting and destruction. How terrible is the specter of an enemy with whom we would have no idea of the basis on which to make a pact! Really it is our viscera, the needs and weaknesses of our flesh, which first of all make possible the recognition of other beings. The body recognizes fellow creatures, but the spirit never. A disembodied intelligence would be pure destructiveness, irrepressible, implacable. It is the organs that tire of the battle and make us conceive a desire for peaceful company, perhaps because of the other's pleasing body or culinary skills. If, some day, we should confront beings with whom we shared no other attribute than the capacity to think, reflective consciousness, it is to be feared that there would be war without quarter, uncompromisingly them or us. It is the body that interposes itself to the haughty, disembodied fury of the spirit. Pure intelligence cannot be dealt with, like the purely spiritual and absolutely *other* God of pre-Christian monotheism. We know that our souls are those pitiless extraterrestrials without entrails, cold, merciless, calculating, whose rigid plans stop at nothing. Within our humble and affectionate earthling body lurks the emotionless Martian for whom other men are no more than beasts of burden, the authoritarian, reasoning Grand Lunar, who recognizes only subjects and victims. There is a sense in which we feel, terrified, how he grows within us. We pretend that we are expecting from outer space a threat that indubitably comes from within, from that inner abyss whose infinite silence would suffice to terrify a thousand Pascals. There, awaiting the hour for the invasion, crouches the implacable, the inhuman thing: that which thinks.

# 8

## LYING IN WAIT
## FOR THE TIGER

Tyger! Tyger! burning bright
In the forests of the night . . .
        William Blake, *Songs of Innocence and Experience*

THOUGH THIS CONFESSION may possibly damage me politically, I must admit that I feel a decided affection for that type of English adventurer, the golden child of imperialism, whose poetic courage discovered (or invented) the marvels of India for a fascinated Europe. It is the type of British soldier or civil servant who appears as a protagonist in many of Kipling's best tales, a hero as incompatible with mere respect for the forms and persons of the colonial milieu in which he lives as the Spaniards were in America, a hero whose heroism consists in being sufficiently impervious to everything around him never to lose his identity and Anglo-Saxon values and sufficiently sensitive to epic beauty to create the legend of the world which he destroys.

There he is, seated at the door of his bungalow, sipping a cup of tea with studied naturalness or meditatively smoking his old briar pipe. The Indian boy who serves him appears on silent feet to collect some croquet mallets that have been left forgotten on the lawn and retires with a murmur of courteous "sahibs" floating on the air. Fifty yards away the jungle is dense and menacing, a damp tangle of thorns; the monkeys' cries have diminished considerably and only the anxious wail of a watchful langur can be heard. As if in answer to it, a spotted deer gives a loud cry of alarm, advising his herd of some undesirable presence nearby. Then, concentrating the heartbeat of the whole jungle with indisputable power, a sort of colossal cough sounds forth, the deep yawn of a giant: "*Aaaaoun! Oooouuun!*" It is the voice of the hunting tiger.

The tiger! There can be no doubt: the tiger and the Englishman are made for each other. In the whole art of hunting, elective affinities have never permitted so obvious a case, a love-hate relationship at first sight with such fruitful adventurous consequences. The great cat has just that mixture of discretion and disreputable dynamism which the Briton has flaunted all over the world. He is a predator who knows how to unite ferocious efficiency with elegance, who raises camouflage to a splendid sumptuousness and makes cruelty a bold miracle of harmony. Nothing is as erroneous as making the lion the symbol of the British nation, for, though I don't wish to detract from that maned creature's merits, his characteristics are much less British than those of the tiger, as is easily ascertained. The lion is lazy and sedentary, the tiger constantly on the move; the lion usually hunts in a group, the tiger is a solitary hunter; the lion seems more imposing and terrible than he really is, while the tiger hides matchless strength under a deceptively soft and fragile appearance; and in particular, the lion rarely becomes fond of human flesh, while the tiger may come to prefer it to any other because it is particularly delicious and easy to obtain. Moreover, the solemn lion may, in any case, be the emblem of the Londoner with his bowler and his umbrella, but the tiger, who is a much more sporting feline, is an infinitely more satisfying representation of the colonial Englishman or the explorer, the Englishman abroad, who is (or has been?) the real Englishman. Both prudent and daring, perfidious and defiant, brutal and velvety, tiger and Englishman looked into each other's eyes with admiration and challenge from the first time that the first British conqueror set foot in India. But the most important thing still remains to be said, and it is that for a born hunter like the Englishman, the man-eating tiger is game to dream about, for he is always ready to change from victim to executioner and turn hunting into a duel; furthermore, the tiger's crimes place him beyond the pale of any society for the protection of animals, and hence hunting him combines the enchantments of sport and the blessings of morality. A man-eating tiger is not hunted, he is executed. What Englishman would be insensible to this sweetly hypocritical collusion of the joys of the hunt with the administration of justice?

A whole hunting literature has arisen to recount the adventures of those hunters who specialize in freeing the world of the menace of man-eaters. It in no way resembles the usual hunting stories which tell how some Anglo-Saxon Nimrod polishes off "a" lion or accounts for "two" rhinoceroses. Here, what is tracked is "the" murderous tiger, whose taste for human flesh has individualized and identified him to the point of taking him out of the anonymity of his species and giving him an authentic personality of his own. By losing his general qualities the beast in some sense also loses his animality and is sinisterly humanized, becoming more like our forest outlaws or wood demons. The animal pursued by the ordinary hunter is a repetition of the species' Platonic prototype, momentarily individualized only by the particular circumstances of the hunt. We can say of every wild beast what Borges wrote of the bison:

> Intemporal, innumerable, zero,
> he is the last bison and the first.

But the man-killer has no right to dilute himself in that flowing zoological impersonality and is marked by a special word that identifies him as clearly as his name itself. The hunter must make sure on every occasion that the tiger he has killed was really "that tiger," the only one, the one sought. Otherwise he would have to start the pursuit all over again. Hence, each hunt becomes a combat with sharply defined characteristics, different from the rest, and each shot that accounts for a man-eater acquires in some sense an exciting aura of homicide. One becomes what one eats; the animal who eats animals keeps his animality, but the beast who knowingly feeds on men (a different case from the beast who occasionally kills a man, for that is simply the chance of the moment) ends by being infected with humanity and his execution takes on the quality of a legal murder, like any other form of the death penalty. The hunter who kills a man-eater in a sense kills a fellow creature. This gives a special quality to this kind of hunting, which resembles a tournament, even a game of chess, in which one enthusiastic murderer seeks another through the indifferent jungle. Both must make use of the same signals, the same clues; both can be betrayed by the same cry of a frightened monkey, or a deer unexpectedly taking flight. Both must know how to camouflage themselves, know how to wait, to be deadly of aim and implacable when the fatal blow is struck. Sleep, weakness of the flesh, fear, or hunger afflict both of them in fundamentally the same way (or at least so it appears in the tales that relate these exploits, which are the ones I am referring to in this chapter; as for the other tiger and the other hunter, "those who are not in the verse," as Borges would say, I know absolutely nothing about them relevant to this case). It is a confrontation of power with power but sealed with the charisma of combat with the dragon, the subjugation of the infernal beast who demands his tribute in innocent human lives, of intelligence and civilization crushing the primordial enemy who, since the dawn of time, prowls around the campfires, who sparkles in the darkness with his hungry eyes and awaits the opportune moment to aim a blow with his terrible claws.

So far I have spoken exclusively of the tiger, but I believe that I must also make mention of that other form of felinity that can become no less addicted than the tiger to delicious human flesh. I refer to the panther, who is apt to alternate with his larger cousin in the role of hated protagonist of the stories that tell of the fight against the man-eaters. The panther often has more treacherous characteristics than the tiger; he is more astute, less honest, given to attacking from behind. What he loses in size he gains in cruel subtlety, in an aptitude for betrayal. Moreover, since his need for food is less than that of the tiger, his taste for human flesh seems always to be marked with the stigma of vice; man seems such a disproportionately large morsel for him that only a gastronomic perversion could tempt him to pursue it. A specific skill defines him in a sinister way—his ability to climb trees, to attack from above. This possibility endows the terrors of the jungle with a third dimension and presupposes another, additional challenge for the hunter, who often chooses the branches of a tree as a refuge or ambush against his enemy. The leopard's deadly lightfootedness, its sinister beauty—which not only fascinates but also perturbs us, like everything that is both beautiful and hostile to us—make this subtiger a peculiarly dangerous enemy, a jungle combination of Iago and Lady Macbeth; for say what you will, my friends, I am convinced that Lady Macbeth must have been stunningly beautiful.

I understand that the classic writer of this literary genre is Jim Corbett, of whose work I have read very little. *My* killer of man-eaters has always been and always will be Kenneth Anderson. I have read few books with as much pleasure as his, which combine the best narrative skills with an ingenuous and contagious love for the field of adventure offered by India. He presents every one of his hunts as a real detective case. In the first place he describes the more or less long list of murders committed by the striped or spotted beast; then he tells us about his initial explorations and tracking efforts; then he puts out a bait animal and takes up his station in a *machan*, concealed in the branches of some tree or in any somewhat protected place; then a tense lying-in-wait, from which the man-eater very frequently flees wounded. The hunter must pursue him, to reach a final encounter and a denouement which is no less emotion-laden for being expected. The story concludes with some lines that usually reveal the animal's physical deformation or the "ethical" reason that led the feline to prefer human flesh as his diet. This pattern is by no means absolutely rigid; there are many descriptions of special peculiarities, tigers with terrifyingly different psychologies, the incidental appearances of brave and long-suffering Hindus, the amusing or terrifying encounters with other representatives of the jungle's fauna. Kenneth Anderson measures out the suspense of his adventures without affectation and has a marvelous capacity for introducing us familiarly into the magical world he frequents. Even the titles of each hunt are exactly right: *The Spotted Devil of Gummalapur, The Killer of Jalahalli, The Hermit of Devarayandurga, The Man-eating Panther of the Yellgiri Hills, The Evil One of Umbalmeru, The Striped Terror of the Chamala Valley.* The personalization of the feline enemy, of which I spoke before, is splendidly accentuated by Anderson, who may either acquire a particular hatred for an intolerably perverted beast or end one of his stories with this reverent paragraph: "The skin of this panther now adorns the hall of my bungalow. I cannot help but record the deep admiration and respect in which I hold this beast. For while others killed in stealth, taking their victims unawares, this leopard fought cleanly and courageously in defense of its own life, against great odds, though it was severely wounded."

If the theory of animal-machines belongs to Cartesian philosophy—as do certain forms of "scientific" mechanicalism—no one is, fortunately, less Cartesian then Kenneth Anderson. I can see him now in one of the photographs that illustrate his books, wearing his hat with the drooping brim and military air, the tips of his reddish mustache standing up like pennants; on his knees rests Nipper, the stray dog who saved his life by warning him of the presence of the spotted devil of Gummalapur when the leopard was about to leap on him from the roof of a native hut; in the background of the picture the first trees, still looking almost tame, mark the beginning of the jungle. He seems to have sat down for a moment to go through the over-ceremonious ritual of the photograph, and to want to be getting up to go to his *machan* and begin his wait, for the call of the *sambar* shows that the tiger has begun to prowl. I think that he is the only man whom I can really say I envy.

# 9

# THE ENDLESS PILGRIMAGE

You have forgotten much, my reader, and yet, as you read these lines, you remember dimly the hazy vistas of other times and places into which your child eyes peered. They seem dreams to you today. Yet, if they were dreams, dreamed then, whence the substance of them?

Jack London, *The Star Rover*

N OT TO BELIEVE in happiness is a form of skepticism that everyone achieves sooner or later. There are people who make great moan about it, but most of us relinquish that emphatic concept with resignation and even with relief. It is like ridding oneself of a badly posed question, of an enticement that justifies in a ghostly way all ethical mortifications, a conjuring trick intimately linked to that fundamental deception, the future. Or to the past? In this case, renunciation is harder to digest. Anyone can abandon the hope of happiness out of indolence or ennui, but when we are assailed by the memory of happiness, by the obsessive episode that seems to be the pith and stimulus of our whole memory, how can we stop thinking about it? Blessed are they who have never been happy—or those who were happy and have forgotten it, always supposing that this is possible—for they will renounce happiness without tears! For my part, I can offer the same confidence that Merleau-Ponty made one day to Sartre: "I shall never recover from my incomparable childhood."

But do not think that I am now going to proclaim myself, without reservations, an upholder of the myth of "golden, happy childhood." In the first place it would be obscene and criminal to try to prove that all childhoods are happy; like Camus, I cannot imagine any fiercer fuel for the rebellious soul than the unbearable injustice of children's pain. In the second place, I know that in my childhood I was happy, but not always or even most of the time. It is possible that my present state of melancholy idealizes my daily routine when I was eight or nine years old and turns any reasonable Saturday afternoon pastime into unimaginable bliss. Nonetheless, I cannot deny one particular and unquestionable period of happiness whose memory is so clear, so detailed, so piercing, that it would be easier for me to doubt one of my present sensations or experiences than to doubt it. My happiness at that time was not an unconscious perfection on which I am reflecting *a posteriori* with amazed envy; contradictory as it may seem—I myself would, in any other case, uphold the opinion which denies the possibility of this experience—my happiness at that time was accompanied by the ecstatic knowledge that I was happy. If, on this point, the impatient reader adjures me to instruct him about what I understand as happiness, I can only refer him to the

definition—better still, the description—of ecstasy written by
Valle-Inclán in his *Lámpara maravillosa*: "It is the joy of being
caught in a circle of pure emotion, which aspires to being eternal. No joy and no terror, comparable to that sensation of the
soul unloosed!" Not only do I remember perfectly the circumstances and images that went along with my fit of happiness—
which was not excessively long, have no fear, only fifteen or
twenty days—but also a number of sensations of taste and
smell, as well as some vague detached-from-the-body feelings
which I doubt my ability to describe in writing.

I was ten years old and had fallen ill with a mild case of
measles. Twenty days' rest in complete isolation were pre-
scribed to keep me from infecting my siblings and schoolmates.
I was settled in my parents' bedroom—psychoanalysts, take
note!—and during that happy period it was my only horizon.
I had almost no fever or other kinds of discomfort; I was not
being threatened with hypodermic injections. Ensconced in my
refuge, I spent all day in bed, chatting sporadically with my
siblings, who cautiously peeked in the door from time to time,
keeping the required distance, and who observed me with envy.
I had my toy sword at hand, a plastic model of the French
battleship *Richelieu*, which for me was the *vera effigies* of Sandokan's *King of the Sea*, and my box of soldiers. I read incessantly; I read two or three books every day, not counting a
dozen or so comic books. Every day my mother brought up
the day's supply of literature. I almost never asked her for a
specific book; she always knew exactly which were best. It was
then that I read Sandokan's last adventures and those of the
Black Pirate; I read Zane Grey's *Valley of Wild Horses* and James
Oliver Curwood's *The Grizzly King*; I read *Puck of Pook's Hill*
and *Plain Tales from the Hills*, by Kipling. One day she brought
me *King Solomon's Mines* and I made the acquaintance of Allan
Quatermain; on another occasion she appeared with two
novels—*The Star Rover* and *Before Adam*—by an author whose
name I heard for the first time, Jack London. It was the old
edition by the Prometeo publishing house, adorned with the
author's wolf-head *ex libris* and translated by Fernando Valera.
Jack London was the greatest discovery of that period in par-

adise. I remember other things: the warm, sweet taste of boiled rice with tomato sauce, a certain way the sun had of filtering through the slats of a blind which I can see perfectly by simply shutting my eyes. At night, when the light was put out, I felt shivers of enjoyment just thinking of the next day; I would mutter, "Tomorrow and day after tomorrow and the day after that too. . . ." It was the first and last time that I welcomed the future without reservations. Occasionally I would leave the book open on the bedspread and close my eyes in an access of bliss so intense that I wanted to cry. A motionless, book-fed, selfish happiness, you will say, made out of isolation and petting. I regret that the memory is not edifying, but I am sure that it was then, and only then, that I felt happy.

I emerged from my quarantine without too much regret, for by then I was beginning to be anxious to see my friends again and play horse races with my brother José. At that time we carried on with some of our school friends a complicated political game with india-rubber soldiers; the night before I was released from my sickbed I received a telegram from the General Staff of one of my neighbors declaring war on me, which contributed vastly and joyfully to shortening my convalescence. But even then I could not hide from myself the fact that what had been offered me during those days was something qualitatively different from and superior to all my other possible joys. I left my castle without overpowering sadness but with the profound conviction that I had at last experienced something irrecoverable. As I have said, Jack London and especially his *Star Rover* were the crowning wonder of those days so prodigal in marvelous discoveries. I cannot think of that author or reread that novel without remembering, with tremendous exactness, my German measles. And that is why I have had to turn aside for a moment to take up the subject of happiness and its irreversible flight, as I prepare to comment on *The Star Rover*.

*The Star Rover* is one of the last novels written by John Griffith London—Jack London—shortly before he broke with the American Socialist party and committed suicide on his Glen Ellen Ranch in California. Not long before, just as he was preparing to occupy it, a fire had destroyed his fantastic Wolf

House, a utopian and feudal structure which he had built at the cost of much effort and money. By this time editors paid little attention to the man who had been the most popular novelist of his time. "I would rather be a superb meteor, every atom of me in magnificent glow, than a sleepy and permanent planet," he had said, summing himself up with rhetorical sincerity. A superb meteor, that is, a stellar wanderer.

As for its narrative structure, *The Star Rover* leaves much to be desired. London did not entirely succeed in balancing the different stories involved in the central tale and let himself be carried away more than he should have by his mania for rambling on and on, which occasionally led him to theorize somewhat unappealingly about evolution and transmigration. London suffered from the same sort of informative obsession as H. G. Wells, apparently characteristic of the socialistic regenerationism of the period, which entranced them and resulted in their giving history or biology lessons suitable for a left-leaning Sunday-school class. But the strength of the novel's structure of ideas is truly incomparable. London creates a literary myth which is in its turn a metaphor of literature itself, or better still, of the need for and the impulse of storytelling. The tale's pseudoreligious or spiritualist interest, to which London and some of his most dogmatic critics assign primary importance, leaves me *almost* as unmoved as do the boring spiritualist disquisitions in Conan Doyle's *The Land of Mist*, in which a Professor Challenger grown older babbles endlessly among ectoplasm and mediums. I emphasize the word *almost* because even on this murky terrain Jack London preserves his magical ability to arouse contagious enthusiasm, which is one of the greatest charms of his narrative style. But as a reflection on the reader's paradoxical condition, on the power and subjection of the imagination, on what stories mean to a person who is condemned to living a fantasy, *The Star Rover* is an unforgettable piece of fiction, a literary adventure. The great storyteller, with the liberation that death represents already lodged in his vitals, tried to express for the last time the key of his dream, the prodigious enigma of the passion for storytelling.

Darrell Standing is awaiting the gallows on Death Row in

the penitentiary at Folsom and summarizes, for the reader and himself, the last part of his life. He has spent eight years in San Quentin as part of his sentence of life imprisonment for murder. A false accusation by another prisoner made him a suspect in having received and hidden some dynamite which was intended to assist a mass escape from the California prison. The governor of San Quentin tries to make him confess where he has hidden the nonexistent explosive; to do so, he subjects him to unbroken solitary confinement and the terrible torture of the jacket. This torture consists of a sort of very tight straitjacket whose pressure squeezes all the body organs and causes terrible pain and a dreadful swelling which can easily cause the sufferer's death. Standing does not confess, for he has nothing to confess, and the governor gradually lengthens the duration of the torture. Following the advice of another prisoner who is also in solitary confinement, with whom he communicates by rapping on the wall in code, Standing learns to make his body insensible to pain until he achieves a sort of voluntary death. Once he has succeeded in doing this, he leaves his carnal envelope behind and relives some of his past existences. The solitary cell and the jacket no longer exist for him, and he finds himself being a hired assassin during the Baroque period in France, a Mormon boy in a wagon train attacked by Indians, and an English sailor cast away in far-off Korea. His torture ceases to have any effect on him and he has nothing but scorn for the governor, who, by trying to act as his executioner, paradoxically becomes his liberator. Standing eagerly desires the jacket instead of fearing it. Thus he can be a shipwrecked sailor who has found refuge on a tiny isle in the Pacific and a Viking who eventually becomes a member of Pilate's guard in the Palestine of Jesus. He can be our remote ancestors, those of whom no memory remains except in that part of our consciousness which we can no longer call ours. An absurd incident with a guard means that he will be condemned to death, but Darrell Standing climbs the steps of the scaffold convinced of his immortality and curious to know what new adventures await his soul in its endless pilgrimage.

London's descriptions of living conditions in San Quentin

prison are worthy of standing beside the great sagas of imprisonment, such as Dostoevski's *The House of the Dead* or Sade's letters. The debasement; the physical degradation; the constant threat of another, even stricter incarceration as punishment for crimes committed in the prison itself; the use of torture as a method of coercion in the American penitentiary system early in this century—all the horror of the repressive devices which society views with a clear conscience—find a relentless poet in this rebel who loves the great open spaces of snow and waves. Further, some of the stories about previous lives which London inserts in *The Star Rover*, such as Adam Strang's adventures in Korea and his long-delayed vengeance, can figure among the most perfect tales of this master storyteller.

The fundamental element in the book, however, is the idea itself of liberation by imaginary means. The soul can be all things, as a Greek once said; a single pattern, a single plot, will never be enough for it. What it loses in availability for action it gains in the capacity for storymaking. What imprisons the star wanderer's body frees him. Imagination is the intelligent use of a fetter, the faculty of surmounting the perpetual shortcomings of our desires by attaining privileged joy. Can a magical use of poverty perhaps change it into riches? It does not seem that imagination operates under any other principle. That social outcast, tied, gagged, all vitality fled, who has deliberately stopped the blood in his veins and suspended his heartbeats, is like you, reader. You too—exactly like me, who now imagine you—have chosen the jacket of the armchair and the crossed legs in order to escape from yourself, to establish yourself in something different, unknown, or improbable. You too refuse the chance to be many and prefer to continue limiting yourself until you turn into a mummy with a book in your hands rather than to renounce forever the many existences that bubble in your dreams. I firmly believe that the doctrine of transmigration of souls had its origin in the vivid incorporation of their hearers into the stories that were told them and the imaginative possibility of endlessly recreating them in the privateness of memory. Reading, by separating access to narration even further from external circumstances, has turned metempsychosis into an everyday experience. After all, transmigration is not a religious deviation that was added to the more or less sensible idea (in former times even a scientific idea) of the soul, but a necessary elucidation of the soul's capacity for eternal change. The soul combines the attributes of impermanence with the very essence of the everlasting; it is changing but invulnerable, subject to the most radical transformations but condemned to endure. Let us remember that the word *psyché* meant, for the Greeks, both "soul" and "butterfly." The butterfly is a metaphor of the soul not only because of its errant flight, an apparent denial of its inexorable trajectory, but also because of its metamorphic nature as worm, chrysalis, and then flying jewel. The absurd thing, if we accept the soul's existence, is not to believe in metempsychosis but to confine absolute psychic mobility within a single option of space and time. But I have already said that I recognize in *The Star Rover* the jubilant affirmation of the storytelling capacity, not a certain heretical kind of religious conviction. This is the proof I advance. In view of the chain of reincarnations and the sensation of sterile weariness that such a multiplication of grief brings to mind, I can conceive of only one valid religious response, the one offered by Buddhism in such a case, proposing as its ultimate aim to emerge from the wheel of karma and attain the meaningless repose of nirvana. But, faced with his infinite deaths and sufferings, prisons and privations, Jack London–Darrell Standing reacts only with insatiable curiosity and that desire for "more and then still more" which characterizes the child seated at the storyteller's feet. The protagonist's body suffers, becomes weary, struggles, dies; but the soul enjoys the delights of a good *plot*.

It was not hard to foresee. When all is said and done, the prisoner in San Quentin who dreams in the quietness of his bonds of all adventures and all loves was another guise of the little boy who read London and Salgari in his sickbed. The first was a symbol of the second, just as this whole chapter is a symbol of this book and of the relationship that makes us brothers, my reader.

# 10

## AMONG THE
## FAIRIES

From inside the hood came a noise as of someone sniffing. . . .
A sudden unreasoning fear of discovery laid hold of Frodo. . . .
The shadow bent to the ground, and then began to crawl toward
him. . . . But at that moment there came a sound like mingled
song and laughter. Clear voices rose and fell in the starlit air. . . .
"Elves!" exclaimed Sam in a hoarse whisper. "Elves, sir!"

J. R. R. Tolkien, *The Fellowship of the Ring*

PERHAPS THE SIMPLEST THING, to begin with, is to say that *The Lord of the Rings* is the most complete literary fantasy of the last fifty years. As we all know—though this is frequently forgotten when it is observed from the narrow fortress of scientism or historicism—literature is free but not exactly fanciful. However, occasionally we accept a work so independent both in subject matter and execution of what is usual at the time of its appearance, so lacking in ambition for stylistic progress, a book which accepts so eagerly the blind alley of a narrative form that has already been exhaustively explored and which confines itself so unashamedly to a subject matter that appears to appeal to very few, that the description of "fantasy" inevitably rises to our lips when we try to describe it. I think that its regressive character is essential to this description of fantasy, and it would be well to remove from the term any evaluative connotation (within the narrow margins of possibility, for all of us are infected with progressivism or no less obsessively assailed by the nostalgia that is its opposite) so as to preserve it as a relevant and distinctive trait in comparison with works which are superficially considered fantasy and which are almost the direct opposite of what is understood by the word I have

.The ElvenKing's Gate.

employed. The deliberateness of the regressive intention, or the renewing intention, are for the moment unimportant. A book like Raymond Roussel's *Locus solus*, for instance, seems to me to be very far from any suspicion of fantasy because it is a truly advanced work, as much from the viewpoint of its complex and obsessive structure—like one of those sets of Russian dolls—as for the cold quality of the story's unfolding. *The Lord of the Rings*, on the other hand, or William Beckford's *Vathek*, are prototypical pieces of literary fantasy, at least according to my previous argument, which may perhaps owe too much to an evolutionary idea of literature. Placing it in this category of "fantasy" literature may tinge the work that receives the name with an aura of superfluity which would be frankly unwelcome, especially insofar as this could give rise to the converse impression that what seems desirable or merely possible is a necessary literary creation.

If I persist in giving Tolkien's work such an ambiguous description—despite the fact that I regretted it as soon as I had used it, as the intelligent reader will have deduced from these painful explanations—it is because it is one way of approaching adequately the peculiarity of the relationship between the reader and *The Lord of the Rings*. This relationship is one of total acceptance or open annoyance. We are in the presence of one of those ten or twelve books which are either unforgettable or a relentlessly boring and childish "tall story." This is the fate of fantasy, in my opinion; either you enter into it or you don't. Since nothing encourages the reading of them—neither questions in momentary vogue nor the stylistic development of writing—literary fantasies are usually also read fancifully. If they touch the chord in the reader which responds to their differentness, no book will produce a more gratuitous and complete satisfaction, simply because it is unexpected. In the opposite case, nothing can reverse the puzzled hostility aroused by these pages, which are at once mannered and completely out of the ordinary. Tolkien is not unaware of this, when he points out in the preface to the book's paperback edition his belief that its only defect lies in being too short. And indeed, the thousand-odd pages of concentrated text in *The Lord of the Rings* leave unsatisfied the reader who has fallen in love with this literary fantasy, who would not be sorry to see it last for at least another thousand pages with as generous a spontaneity as in the first thousand; on the other hand, the reader who doesn't like it will find the first hundred pages unbearably detailed, and the whole work a sort of apotheosis of excess.

The worst—or the best, according to one's opinion—of literary fantasies is that no cultural alibi justifies the labor of reading them, merely the reader's whim, the simple desire to do so. There is no lack of historical or ethical reasons to enjoin even those who are least fond of Tolstoy to lose themselves in the exhausting meanderings of *War and Peace*, but giving oneself over to *The Lord of the Rings* can have no other motive than the joy received by reading it. Once we are won over by Tolkien there is no reason to abandon him or to wish that the story with which he has entranced us might be shorter. But we are dealing with an exceptionally complete literary fantasy, because millions of readers—and not the worst readers by any means— have recognized their own fantasies in Tolkien's and have passed through the dark or radiant landscapes of Middle-earth as through their long-yearned-for native land. What seemed destined for the approbation of a few eccentrics immediately won over a multitude, from brainy Oxford dons who bent over their colleague's work with delighted astonishment to California "hippies" who decorated their jackets with buttons reading "Frodo lives." Tolkien's fantasy has had much better acceptance than he himself expected, probably, when he wrote it.

*The Lord of the Rings* has been described as the longest fairy tale in the world, a characterization which I think is not far off the mark. This great length, which as I have said the true enthusiast will not deplore, is in my opinion one of the keys to the book's undoubted narrative success. The story line is so simple, its ethics so direct and conventional—Light versus Darkness, Honor versus Baseness, Friendship versus Hatred, Beauty versus Hideousness—that any summary would relegate it to the most brain-numbing triteness. Told in fifty pages, it would merely be another edition of a fairy tale that we have heard told a thousand times before, with this or that set of details. But the book's achievement is precisely *not* to refer us directly to that fairy kingdom inhabited by orcs, goblins, and wizards, talking trees, and wolves that prowl by night, whose more or less generic conventions are preserved in our memories among other recollections redolent of hot cereal and mothballs. Tolkien tells us everything as if it were being told for the first time. He answers all the questions that children are apt to ask when they hear a story: what the dwarves' city was like—house by house—what the name of the prince's sword was, how many friendly eagles there were, what wizards ate, what had happened before the story began, what the names of the places were where the travelers went and what they looked like, how the orcs were dressed and where they lived, and so on. And when he explains these details he never lets himself be carried away by the unlikely or the unnecessarily extravagant. Once the fantastic element has been postulated, Tolkien makes the discreetest possible use of it. Foreseeing our reluctance, after much previous disillusionment, to enter the world of the marvelous all at once, he makes it tolerable for us gradually. We feel at home, but not altogether; we recognize the things around us, but only up to a point. One critic has described it very well: "familiar but not too familiar, strange but not too strange."[1] But the presence of the ordinary, described in the most realistic terms, predisposes us to accept the magic element, whose appearance is never more portentous than is strictly necessary. Thanks to its great length, the story slips past with all the leisureliness demanded by Tolkien's deliberate enjoyment of details and the unhurried attention he bestows on each incident in the story. But, and this is perhaps the greatest virtue of Tolkien's style, once his overall design is accepted he cannot be criticized for dwelling too long on things. He never loses the sense of action, nor does he obstruct it to the point of breaking the rhythm of events. Over so many pages, not to lose the narrative pulse is no small achievement, and in my opinion it redeems many of Tolkien's undoubted shortcomings as a writer. Something whose plot alone promised no more than a simple Manichaean tale with fairies as part of the scenery has become, thanks to his skilled prolixity, a fascinating reading experience. It is like reading an ancient magico-epic Celtic poem retold by Dickens or Rider Haggard.

Admirable patience is employed in inventing a sort of lost continent, with all its details of language, history, geography, and folklore, to form a suitable background for the old story of St. George and the dragon. Tolkien's mythology is fundamentally simple and connects with extremely familiar sources. Sauron, the Dark Lord, is—even in his name with its overtones of "saurian"—a new version of the biblical Old Serpent, whose ambition and pride caused him to fall from his radiant condition among the cherubim to the degraded status of a demon tempter. And in his service are all the frightful creatures who somberly press in upon the pure fantasy of fairy tales—dark, faceless specters with blood-chilling laughter, brutally ferocious cannibal orcs, packs of giant wolves whose eyes perturb the shadows around campfires, wizards perverted by an excess of knowledge. Against this sinister brotherhood the eternal characters who represent the Good join forces—dwarves who are industrious and peaceful but not lacking in courage; beneficent fairies, wizards whose goodness is both powerful and wise, haughty princes with shining swords, elemental spirits of woods and rivers.

Among these last the most important are the elves, the free people of woods and hills hymned by Shakespeare and Kipling, the quintessence of untrammeled, sunny, profoundly harmonious life, with no other standard of morality than fleetness and beauty, no other work to do than the manufacture of marvelous playthings with which to intensify their joyous wanderings. Exempted by their enviable condition from the pressing anxieties of history, which for them are merely pretexts for beautiful songs, they exemplify everything that is essentially opposed to the Dark Lord's obsession with enslaving rule, but they are also opposed to the human champions' aggressive desires for justice. They take part in the War of the Ring only when the menace of Sauron casts its ominous shadow even on their idyllic existence, but in fact they do not belong to the realm of politics and their heroism lacks the impassioned door-die touch that characterizes the heroism of men. Their courage flows naturally, unemphatically.

In general, Tolkien's preferences lie with the characters who have been only minimally contaminated by contact with history: the elves, the ents, Tom Bombadil, even the hobbits themselves, yanked only by a quirk of fate out of their rustic, provincial mediocrity, where birthday parties and mushroom-hunting expeditions are the most memorable events. The idealized world of knightly deeds, sublime sacrifices, and flashing swords is a sort of dream which in the end always leaves a bitter taste in the mouth. After all, it is power and dominion that are at stake, and the ambition that lusts for them is merely human madness. It is preferable that those who win should be capable of greater generosity within their greed for power, but the dispute itself belongs to the area of the illusory and unhappy, no matter how much heroism it engenders. The noblest warrior is always on the edge of a demonic seizure that will place him on the side of the dark powers—thus Boromir's treason and the madness of Denethor. Even Aragorn shines at times with a somber glow, and Sam's common sense found something profoundly disturbing about him from their first encounter. The important thing is to achieve a rapid reestablishment of the natural order which allows everyone to forget about affairs of state and relegate great deeds to the role of subjects for epic lays—this is the difference between the Good King and the Dark Lord, for if the latter had triumphed, the inhabitants of Middle-earth would have been immersed in history forever. The elves and ents take part in the conflict much more to help preserve nonhistory than to correct history; and the extreme case is Tom Bombadil, who is so absolutely ahistorical, so primitive and telluric, that he cannot even *understand* what is at stake in the War of the Ring or participate in it on the side of the forces of good. If he were given the Ring, as is suggested at one point, he would lose it. It is nothing that he can appreciate, hide, or preserve. He has no relationship with it and hence does not become invisible when he puts it on, as do all the other creatures. There is something that lies beyond the whole controversy over power, something that takes no part in this struggle, not even to avoid falling under an unjust rule; and that something is, in a way, the best defense against Sauron. For the Ring is not simply power in its most neutral—or let us say administrative—aspect, but the awful fascination of power, that profound and perhaps in some sense incurable corruption of the will which not only the real Empire, but even the coveted shadow of the Empire, brings into being. Except for Bombadil, all who touch the Ring are infected by the noxious urge for domination, and are on the way to becoming human remnants like Gollum or evil spirits like Sauron. Frodo can never again adapt to the peaceful and innocent life of the Shire. Haunted by the ghost of the Master he was on the point of becoming, or in a sense did become, the tortured anguish of his sleepless eyes would have ended by making him the Dark Lord's legitimate and unhappy heir. Those who fought for the ahistorical reestablishment of the natural order never really experienced it again, for the wounds of the war for power cannot be healed and eventually make everything that is not power impossible. After all, the defeated Sauron infected his bitterest enemies with his own curse, and who knows if he did not win the contest in the end.

One of the most curious sensations experienced by the reader of *The Lord of the Rings* is that of finding himself enclosed in a completely moral space. This is perhaps the book's greatest peculiarity and the one which best defines it, for good or ill. By a completely moral space I understand an area where no neutral or ethically irrelevant events occur, and where good or evil inclination of the will is the ultimate cause determining all that happens, the outcome of a battle as well as the configuration of a landscape or the invulnerability of a mail coat. We need not remind ourselves that the usual naturalistic narration, even the most moralizing and exemplary, restricts the scope of the moral to human intentions, while objects both natural and artificial stay in expectant neutrality, and even if they are in the last instance steered toward the good by providence or by the stratagems of reason, they function morally only at an instrumental level.

In *The Lord of the Rings* the moral condition imbues every-thing, and odors, swords, or mountains are first of all good or bad, have taken sides morally just like people, and in the last resort that choice is what determines their effectiveness. All the physical laws are made subject to the supreme law of moral courage, and the operation of causality is above all axiological. This superendowment of meaning with which every move-ment, every tree, or every foodstuff is loaded, contrasts subtly and powerfully with the apparently naturalistic descriptive tone of the narration, changing its realism into something funda-mentally magical. This is the reason we make such an unsur-prised transition from the ordinary to the magical in Tolkien's world. A marvel acquires a certain air of naturalness because naturalness itself is supernatural and marvelous, because the most "physical" reality does not function according to the blind mechanical laws of matter but in accordance with the confused and irreducibly free dictates of the spirit.

All of Middle-earth is the chessboard for the contest between Good and Evil, but each square and each piece on that board, as well as the board itself, are fundamentally *made* of good or evil will—they are not their simple instruments. The result of the combat is doubtful only in appearance; in reality it is decided in advance. To express it by parodying Kant, the final victory is inscribed analytically, not synthetically, in the combat itself. The Good is certainly stronger, and as such must *always* prevail in victory; the fact is that it is more indolent, less active than Evil. The choice of evil will is more intense than that of good will, but it is undercut by weakness at its very root. Tolkien's historical vision is cyclical; a vigorous nucleus of Good gains control of Evil, only to languish later and become imprisoned in a sort of enervation of which the ferocious intensity of Evil takes advantage, to grow and grow until the heart of Good acquires new energy and again binds Evil in chains. To develop all its power, Good needs to be activated, and perhaps in the last instance this is Evil's function in the harmony of the world—that of serving as a provocation for the Good to decide to put forth all its energy.

In each concrete confrontation of the two kinds of will described in *The Lord of the Rings*, it is always the clothing, the weapons, the foods, or the war cries of Light which defeat their somber rivals with their strength. The Good is the standard of efficacy and usefulness, a transcendent counterpart of the classic Anglo-Saxon opinion that makes efficacy and usefulness the criterion of the Good. Hence Frodo, very close to the end of his quest, surrounded by enemies in the very heart of Sauron's territory, succeeds in resting peacefully on the night when he sees his mission and the whole War of the Ring as a simple incident within an infinite and recurrent conflagration which the Good has won in advance, precisely because the universe is ultimately moral and there is nothing stronger than the will for good. There, in the heart of Mordor, the fundamental weakness of the mighty Dark Lord is revealed to Frodo for a moment.

If the positive protagonists of *The Lord of the Rings* were capable of being always and in every case faithful to their will for good, Tolkien's book would lose all its plot and would be the chronicle of an uninterrupted victory. But Evil's great sleight-of-hand trick is to make Good doubt its strength, to undermine its courage with the tempting specter of the possibility of defeat. The spectacle of Evil, that intense frailty, causes the incorruptible strength of Good to waver, to the point of making it forget its necessarily victorious vocation; its triumphant nature plays with the almost unimaginable possibility of *falling*. No murderous specter, no monster risen from Avernus can really affect to the least degree righteous will, its concerns, or its works, much less prevail against them. The only wound that Darkness can inflict on Light is the shadow of doubt about the always triumphant strength of Light itself. All the immense and desperate intensity of Sauron's evil will, and that of his servants, is turned toward taking advantage of this moment of weakness. But they are constant victims of the adverse results of their evil will, which always ends by aiding their enemies. They are condemned to do good while attempting evil, as Randel Helms demonstrates in an excellent analysis of this question.[2] The positive qualities of evil will—Sauron's wisdom and political astuteness, the fidelity of some of the orcs to orders received—in the end act against Evil, precisely because they themselves are positive. The evil characters are betrayed no less by their capacities than by their deficiencies. The only effective weapon left to Evil is its own spectacle, the anguish which its desolate image provokes in the good characters. Within the Good, the poisonous suspicion of the possibility of a victory by Evil grows and grows, nourished exclusively by the irrepressible intensity of the perverse presence. "The Paladin's heart trembled like the leaf on a tree, not because the serpent had caused him a wound but because it made him feel such horror and loathing that he trembled despite himself, moaned, and even bewailed being alive. Meanwhile, frantic and uncaring, he was traversing the darkest paths, the worst places of that tangled wood. . . ." (Ludovico Ariosto, *Orlando furioso*.)

This totally moral space in which the War of the Ring takes place and the consequent victory of upright will mark the essential difference between Tolkien's mythology and Lovecraft's. Both of them share a certain elemental imagery of abominable subterranean creatures or things infected with evil. But Lovecraft is not moral because he is not a Manichaean, despite August Derleth's efforts to muddy the waters in order to reform him in this respect: for Lovecraft only Evil is strong, only it is in a certain sense *real*, while the Good is an illusion, the fruit of ignorance, a postponement of the inevitable, a truce that horror mysteriously concedes before it triumphs forever. In the last instance, the very notions of Good and Evil lack cosmic meaning; they are simple examples of approbation or disapproval which frail human creatures project upon a universe ignorant of their existence, and upon colossal Entities unimaginably different from men, whose plans either exclude or enslave them. Maybe there are certain norms in the universe that restrain or control the power of the Great Elder Ones, but they must be as obviously remote from what men call the Good as the menacing entities themselves. Lovecraft's heroes are crushed by their confrontation with the infinite, and can count neither on their energy nor their virtue; their only positive function is to refuse to collaborate with the monsters and their idolaters, or at most to cautiously slow down their maneuvers

in an effort to postpone the inevitable victory as long as possible.
But they must pay very dearly for this work of resistance, this
*maquis* against horror, and most of them end their venture in
madness, in suicide, or in terrorized anticipation of the great
winged shadow as it approaches their windows. What more
could they wish for than to be able to depend on swords forged
by magicians to defeat all evil, on war cries that their enemies
cannot endure, on shining phials that make the shadows recede!
But the elves never come to their rescue.

Undoubtedly the twisting staircases, the odors of corruption,
and the abominable voices or inscriptions that overshadow
Lovecraft's tales have inspired the creation of Mordor, as well
as that declaration of Gandalf's in which he admits that in the
deep caverns under Middle-earth there are indescribable things:
"Even Sauron knows them not." But there is no lack of other
precedents. G. K. Chesterton says that within the confines of
the world is a tree that is both more and less than a tree, and
"a tower, perhaps, of which the very shape was wicked." And
even earlier—I was surprised never to see it mentioned in
connection with Tolkien—arises Robert Browning's poem
*Childe Roland to the Dark Tower Came,* in which we find the
sinister tower, "blind as the fool's heart," the burned-out, ominous landscape, the knight who fords a river fearing to trample
the face of some corpse or feel his foot getting entangled in the
hair or beard of a drowned man, the convention of dead heroes
at the end, and the slug-horn's defiant blast. But perhaps Tolkien's most specific contribution is precisely that magical and
victorious reinforcement of goodness which Lovecraft's pessimistic fatalism cannot admit: the deepest message of *The Lord
of the Rings* may well be an exhortation not to let oneself be
crushed by the apparent invulnerability of evil.

In *The Lord of the Rings* there is a marked predominance of
decadence which I find especially relevant. Good as well as evil
seems to have degenerated in Middle-earth; whether it speaks
of wizards, landscapes, champions, or apparitions, Tolkien's
book is always the chronicle of decline. Warriors set out for
combat grown old and exhausted, heirs of a glorious tradition
that weighs heavily upon them; in their splendid isolation the

ents sigh for their lost entwives and fade away without issue; even the elves live more in the past than the present, and the old king Théoden harangues his knights to ride forth for the last time. But Sauron too is only a shadow of his past malignity and returns to the fray after having been twice defeated, losing one of his fingers, and without the Ring on which his power rests. And at last, victims of an inexpressible melancholy which marks their fate, the victors of the War of the Ring board a ship that will carry them away forever from that Middle-earth which has mysteriously become intolerable to them. Good as well as Evil, victory as well as defeat, undergo the same slow but inexorable process of deprivation, of fading away, of all-pervading nostalgia. Time rebels against them, against their possibility and their confrontation, saps them until the imaginary roots that sustain them crumble away.

In some sense, *The Lord of the Rings* takes place after the golden age of all its characters, negative as well as positive ones. Only the hobbits' bourgeois simplicity has not yet been put to the test; and it falls to them to recover for a moment the outworn tradition of heroism, wisdom, and horror that has completely undermined the other races' vitality. Sam, Merry, and Pippin, who started off from the Shire like childish vacationers with adolescent dreams of glory, return fully grown, transformed into real champions of proven courage; but the golden spontaneity of their better days has ended, and now they can only wait for death to turn the burden of their lordly status into legend. As for Frodo, his long contact with the very heart of history allows him neither rest nor personal hope; from the beginning of his journey he forms part of the brotherhood of those higher beings, exhausted by knowledge and exile, like Gandalf, like Aragorn, even like Sauron himself. For him there will be no Shire again, no cheerful return to birthday parties. It is not difficult to relate this imaginary decadence to the last glimpses of the myth of a green preindustrial England, covered little by little with smoking factories and thrust headlong into a glorious imperial history from which it will emerge triumphant but with wounds that are necessarily mortal. This is an obsession that Tolkien shares with some of his friends, like the

Anglo-Catholic writer C. S. Lewis, whose work can, not un-
reasonably, be related to Tolkien's.[3] But it seems neither fair
nor justifiable to downgrade *The Lord of the Rings* to a kind of
antiprogressive allegory, which it undoubtedly is *also*. What
has declined has been the fairy tale itself, and Tolkien proves
this by raising it to its highest power. Fruits of a kind of storytelling that is outdated but still extremely beautiful, the characters of Middle-earth experience the fading of the magic and
ethical concept that gave them birth. Along with the elves, it
is the crude confrontation of Good with Evil that dies out, in
the neutral physical space that science explores and imposes on
docile common sense. In the end Tolkien's piece of fantasy is
shown to be impossible; he too, like the obsessed Gollum, may
well cry for his "precious," for his lost treasure of elemental
nobility and free-ranging imagination.


ADDENDUM

Sometime it might be worthwhile to study the *graphic* influ-
ences in Tolkien's work, which is so deliberately and consis-
tently visual. Let us recall that Tolkien himself is an excellent
hand at drawing and has personally illustrated one very nice
edition of *The Hobbit*. There can be no doubt of the obvious
pictorial quality of a number of scenes in *The Lord of the Rings*,
which the reader remembers after having read them like stills
from a film of animated drawings. (To be sure, what a marvelous animated film could be made out of the novel!) The most
notable influence is that of the great classic British illustrators
of the early part of this century, like Arthur Rackham, creator
of the illustrations in a book as Tolkienian in feeling as *The
Rhinegold and the Valkyrie*, or the very notable Kay Nielsen.
Tolkien's graphic imagination is decidedly symbolist, even Pre-
Raphaelite. A painter like Burne-Jones, who studied theology
in that same Oxford where Tolkien was later to spend his life,
is the author of paintings that seem like illustrations for the
adventures of the elves; for example, *The Baleful Head*, in which
Perseus is showing Andromeda the Medusa's head reflected in

the waters of a little pool. The scene irresistibly recalls the moment when Galadriel shows Frodo Sauron's baleful eye reflected in the waters of her magic mirror. The elves seem designed after models from Dante Gabriel Rossetti, or even Richard Dadd.

# II

## STRANGER IN
## SACRAMENTO

We swept over the green prairie like a hurricane, and it was a
real delight to see Old Wabble's long white hair, and Old Sure-
hand's still longer brown hair, flying in the wind. . . .

Karl May, *The Desert Island*

I REMEMBER A RADIO SERIAL that I must have listened to when I was nine or ten years old, called *Dos hombres buenos*, with a script written by the gallant José Mallorquí. One of the two protagonists, a Portuguese named João Silveira or something like that, had a special ability or innate magnetism that made him attract fights whenever he stepped into a saloon in any godforsaken Texas town. Five minutes after ordering his whiskey, some bully would come up to him with insulting, challenging words. Silveira never got flustered; confident in his mastery of the quick draw, he would reply softly, "When you say that smile, so I'll know you're not serious. . . ." The fight was not long in coming, and the bully was soon convinced that it would have been wiser to smile while he still had teeth to

smile with. Silveira's roguish statement, which pretends to offer a possible way to avoid a fight but really brings one on, has been engraved on my mind as the symbol of a whole literary genre, the one that turns on the colonization of the North American West. The Portuguese's trademark contains both brashness and courtesy; it is malicious but brave; it pays lip service to leniency but wraps it in a challenge. In some sense these traits are valid for all Western novels. We must work out a defense of "genre" literatures, like detective fiction, Westerns, novels of science fiction or terror, which have been condemned by Hermann Broch to the limbo of *kitsch*. The stories of this genre have a false plot; that is, their true plot is the very convention that defines them as a genre. When someone pronounces the opinion that all Westerns or all detective stories are alike he is formulating a definition, not a criticism, of the genre literatures. They are all alike—in a certain sense they are all the same novel—because they essentially deal with a single theme, deliberately and ritually confined to a certain form whose infinite repeatability is what is truly fascinating for the enthusiast.

What the reader of these genre novels likes, fundamentally, is the fact that they are all alike yet nevertheless undeniably different, and not only in circumstantial details. The same thing is true of all the days of our lives. Something identical endlessly returns, an insoluble conflict, an essential nucleus of meaning, a happy archetype which, rather than coming into our imagination from outside, seems to find itself inside it from the outset; but this repetition carries with it a constant flow of differences, a variation that is all the more overwhelming because it modulates upon a single register.

This vivid contrast, of the different upon a background of sameness, is the strength of genre literatures. The work of genius, among any of them, is the one that achieves the highest point of originality and difference without ceasing to bring a new contribution to the essential nucleus of the genre's conventions. *Don Quixote*, in comparison with the novels of chivalry, is the most obvious example of this. Broch condemns genre novels as *kitsch* because they aspire too obviously and crudely to cause an effect; but this overweening impatience (to keep immediately the promise of bringing a new contribution to the expected plot archetype) is essential to heighten the reader's delight in the difference which will constitute the plot's incidental peculiarities. Naturally all these genres are full of clichés, of stereotypes, of formulas; but the reader who cannot endure mannered writing is not capable of enjoying literature, and a hundred classic and entirely "individual" books would suffice for him to reach the summit of the culture required in the literary sphere. What would become of Shakespeare and Kafka without mannered writing? Genre literatures show us that every situation is literally inexhaustible, that a period, a geographical detail, a homicide, or carnal usages (in the case of one of the most prototypical genres, the erotic novel) are sufficient to define a textual microcosm with disconcertingly inexhaustible possibilities. Genres are born from a fully conscious and artificial decision by three or four talented imitators, and die from a combined lack of interest—it would be rash to decide who tires first—on the part of writers and their audiences. They are neither eternal nor immutable; in this, as in everything, we must be nominalists.

The only genre that arises with the origin itself of literature is the erotic genre; it is not easy to accept the fact that it will some day disappear, but this possibility cannot be excluded *a priori*. Tales of terror are almost as old, and their disappearance is no less improbable, but no less possible. What should our state of mind be when we imagine a humanity freed from the fears of body and soul alike, purged of alluring beauty as well as of the monstrous, a humanity that has forgotten both Dracula and Moll Flanders? Westerns cannot aspire to this longevity bordering on the eternal. There is a sense in which their time has passed, and soon they will constitute a genre restricted to curious scholars, as the Byzantine novel is today.

In addition to a particular historical and geographical setting (the territories of the western United States of America during the nineteenth century and early years of the twentieth), the generic convention also includes elements more vaguely descriptive but no less distinctive than their dates and places—the great semideserts of the plains where the cactus raises its inhospitable arms against an overpoweringly blue sky, the vast ranges where the reddish long-horned cattle graze, the rocky mesas with their unmistakable silhouettes, the little towns with their wooden houses and porches and the saloons with their swinging double doors. A gallery of stereotyped characters, as unchanging and filled with secret meaning as the major arcana of the Tarot—the solitary cowboy who arrives from no one knows where with no possessions but his revolver and his horse, the old swindler with his beaverskin cap, the tall pistol-toter with his craggy face and black outfit, the sheriff who is venal and corrupt but still capable of a last heroic act, the cardsharper, the powerful and unscrupulous stockman who is the unchallenged boss of the town, the saloon hostess who sings like a fallen angel, the noble and sententious Indian chief, the tribe's cruel medicine man, the rancher's spirited, impulsive daughter, the doctor who is a hopeless alcoholic but ready when the time comes to be on the hero's side. One can also count on the well-defined personalities of certain fetishes, like the "Colt," the "Winchester," the old four-horse stagecoach, the broad-brimmed Stetson, the buffalo, the lonely cowboy's swift and intelligent steed, the great silver spurs.

Stories that are put together from these ingredients have a certain pleasant rural and untamed air which does not exclude a clear reference to the birth of cities. Their charm is owed in good measure to the fact that they belong to a past so immediate that anyone can prolong the lines of force which arise from it, and which stretch into our present. It is flattering to imagine that the right to live in cities was won by such purely epic adventures; certainly it ought to have been so, but that was not all of it. Western stories oscillate between enthusiasm for what was being born and a nostalgia sometimes resembling remorse for what had to be sacrificed in order to hasten the birth. Not only are Indians and buffalo massacred, but that dreamy, justice-loving horseman himself is eliminated or disposed of—a horseman who is usually shown to be incapable of accumulating property as the budding civilization requires.

The heroes of Western novels are not—and this is significant—the ones who really did the job; the conquest to which they are said to have contributed certainly left them out. In some sense they slowed the development that brought the West to where it is now, instead of helping it; that was what their heroism consisted of, and it is interesting to see that our present-day disenchantment recognizes this. The monopolistic stockman and the cardsharper who control the town with a Mafia of henchmen at their service and spend their time in bureaucratic intrigue with the property deeds of mines—these are the really civilized people, who are preparing that future which forms our present.

In every rumination on the origin of modern cities there is a melancholy element, when we remember that the epic effort which created them triumphed by disappearing itself. The Western epic fought a nearly impossible fight to achieve conditions in which the epic element was no longer necessary. But the melancholy becomes a feeling of more intense frustration— more exciting too, perhaps—when we realize that the autonomous development of the city obliges us to live in such a way that the epic is absolutely necessary if we are not to be totally devoured, with the aggravating factor that courage has become something rather less obvious than in the times of the city's foundation. It is then that we remember, with idealizing fervor, the indomitable cowboy who never learned to live with the falsity that ruled the burgeoning cities and fought to defend his right not to know, a right that all of us have lost today.

The classic Western writer par excellence is Zane Grey, in whose vast production we can find all the examples of plots, situations, and characters which will return endlessly in the disciples of his school. If Karl Jaspers could say that all of Western philosophy is merely footnotes to the Platonic dialogues, we could state with even greater truth that almost all contemporary Western stories are paraphrases of models first set down by Zane Grey. Though his style is a bit slow and the sentimental episodes he perpetrates are something less than bearable, there is no doubt that he deeply loved the dream of freedom and courage that the word *West* stands for, and he succeeded in transmitting that love to an inexhaustible offspring of readers. The realism of his narrative, so rich in local color, gives us a surprisingly pleasant familiarity with the heroes of his stories, which does not diminish their stature but does make them believable and attractive. Even when he becomes tiresomely informative he maintains the charm of the person who is telling marvelous tales before an avid circle of listeners, and who, to increase his hearers' enthusiasm, hides his own under the guise of carefully neutral accuracy. I feel sure that his pages have delighted John Ford and Howard Hawks, mythically establishing for them the landscape and the men they were later to film. Without Zane Grey it would be hard to imagine *My Darling Clementine* or *Cheyenne Autumn*. Though we had no other reason to be grateful to him than this, it would be enough to constitute an overwhelming debt to this New York City dentist.

Personally, my preferences in the genre have always inclined toward Karl May, a much more supple and imaginative storyteller than Grey, though with a less documentary quality. The West of Karl May is a moving-picture West *avant la lettre*, but a movie made anywhere but in the West. However, he possesses a bewitching ability to spin exciting adventures and has that enviable rhythmic sense necessary to transcribe action in a sufficiently literary way. A large part of his success lies in the amusing qualities of his characters: Old Shatterhand, a pluperfect and somewhat ingenuous German wanderer in American territories, who represents the author's idealized memories of childhood; the sober, brave, impassioned Winnetou, the prototype of the "good Indian," an Apache whose predictable dignity does not lack an element of real charm; the cohort of old swindlers or buffalo hunters who appear in all his stories— quarrelsome, hypochondriacal, always facetious, they as often decide the outcome of a battle by their intervention as bring on disaster with some crazy action. Then there are the dangerous "bad guys," terribly bad, the ones it is hard to get rid of, for they have the bad habit of reappearing when one thought they had been buried a hundred pages before. Once the reader of Karl May accepts the elemental nature of the passions that fuel the plot, he finds himself in the marvelous state of mind of the perfect literary adventure buff—he knows that something is going to happen on every page, and that that "something" could be anything. I can remember having spent a whole summer literally caught in the clutches of Karl May and the characters of his life-sized West. The chapter on the death of Winnetou, for example, despite his treasonable conversion to Christianity, represented one of the strongest literary emotions of my youth. That silent, brave Indian had become obscurely necessary to me.

There is yet another type of Western literature in which the convention has become entirely mechanized, and stylistic resources have been reduced to what is absolutely indispensable for making the author understood—cheap novels, which cost a few cents when I was ten years old, with covers in glaring colors, produced in assembly-line fashion, tearless epics by such authors as Marcial Lafuente Estefanía, José Mallorquí, and Silver Kane. I shamelessly admit having had a wonderful time with "The Coyote," and that tall, dust-covered stranger who swept the lawless town clean of evildoers, dispatching them with an infallible shot between the brows, and then turned out to be a ranger. They are to the novels of Zane Grey and Karl May as the made-for-television films of *Bonanza* and *The Virginian* are to *Stagecoach*, but there is room for everything under the sun, and man dies sooner when deprived of epics than when he slakes his thirst with fourth-rate sagas. The messenger boy who spasmodically reads *The Stranger Came to Sacramento* amid the rumblings of the subway is also the recipient of glory and adventure. I see him in a corner of the train, under his arm the alien but indispensable portfolio full of papers, freckle-faced, his brows knitted with effort and his lips silently forming the words that tell of Texas and of buffaloes. The train pulls in at his station and he does not notice, for he is sunk in a mythical contemplation which knows nothing of insurance policies or urban rentals: "The saloon doors swung open to permit the entrance of a tall, thin man, covered with dust. He looked slowly around at the silent customers who had left their drinks on the counter, and said in a clear, quiet voice, 'Something here smells like a coward.' No one answered. He stepped toward the bar, with his arms hanging loosely at his sides. . . ."

# 12

## WHAT IT MEANS
## TO TREMBLE

O my soul, come in softly,
for I am dying of fear.
                    Anonymous, Spanish 16th century

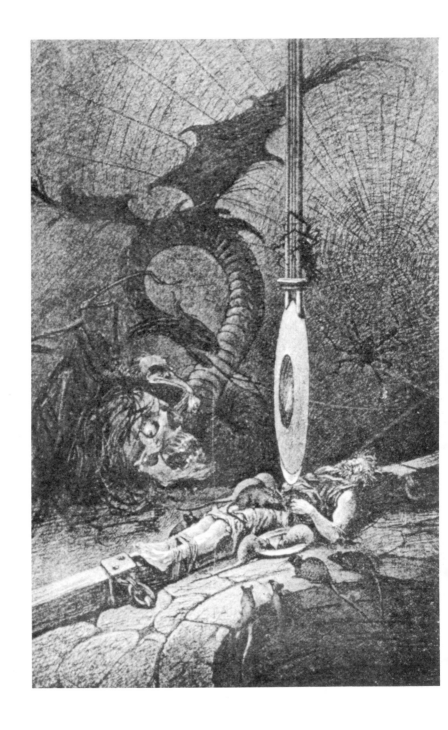

W E WHO ARE FANS of terror tales form an especially obsessed and closed fraternity, as distrustful of those strange "normal" beings who think that Poe is a detective-story writer and are ignorant even of Lovecraft's nationality as we are cordially fraternal to those who share our taste for the shudders. Few literary enthusiasms mark a person as this one does; it is a preference that is not likely to go unpunished.

The true enthusiast of the genre is not an occasional reader of horrifying little tales bought in the penury of a railway-station newsstand or tolerated in the carefree repose of summer vacations; nor has he anything to do with that professional of good taste who courteously appreciates the macabre romanticism of *The Fall of the House of Usher* or condescends to broaden his culture with a few pages of Lord Dunsany or Ambrose Bierce, who are respectable literary figures after all. No, the man who can go a whole week without reading spine-chilling tales, who is not prepared to condemn his aged parents to indigence and sell off his imploring wife and tender babes as slaves if only he can get the money to buy the complete works of Arthur Machen, the man who does not adore certain authors of the genre whose literary perfection is nil but who sprinkle their stories to the swooning-point with somber castles and tireless vampires, the person who does not prepare to read a good werewolf story with the same excited deliberation with which a man who has at last succeeded in getting himself shut up in the same room with the woman of his dreams plans the ultimate details of his attack—that person is a mere *parvenu* of the shudder, a dilettante of anguish, a lukewarm and casual frequenter of the promenades of fear.

Strictly speaking, the horror story is THE TALE par excellence, the prototypical story that we expect to hear when we sit with ears wide open at someone's feet, looking into the flickering firelight; it is the story that, by definition, deserves to be told. We are dealing here with a genre which eschews declamation or fulsome recitation, preferring to slide along in a whisper. This reveals its relationship to the primordial essence of the story, an expressive and fundamentally nocturnal mode, as inappropriate to high-sounding language as to pedantry. Both love and this sort of tale are framed in silence and whispered murmurings. Once the voice has been lowered, in the expectant near-silence filled only with the strange creakings of things that are not quite asleep, how can we resist the temptation to conjure up the ghosts that never leave us, to blaspheme (very much under our breath) against reason and its order, to summon up the elemental panic which our hard-working day or our fear of madness causes us to conceal until nightfall? Just for a moment we suspend the healthy hypocrisy that certifies us as sensible and enterprising citizens of countries buttressed by the progress of science and again see ourselves as we really are: inhabitants of the improbable, residents of nothingness, protagonists of a nightmare so devastating and forlorn that the only way we can preserve our sanity is to try to forget our wretched state insofar as we can. The dead whom we had incontinently thrust out of our sight before they began to frighten us come out of their tombs and show us their repulsive living putrefaction, refusing that quiet disappearance to which we consign them with frightened solicitude; they return conscious of the worm that gnaws them, as Blake said. Faced with this ominous return of the spectral, the good people, those the world's progress depends on—healthy minds, livers in excellent working condition—retreat toward sanity, gasping for fresh air, sun, and butterflies. But there is no lack of frantic creatures, viciously conscious of their own shudders, who once they have experienced the lash of the hair-raising sensation cannot get along without it and return incessantly to the authors who can best offer it to them. Among these twilight beings, gentle reader, I have the misfortune to be included.

The disproportionateness and violence of this pursuit does not fail to arouse astonishment among those who do not suffer from it, and who frequently turn to us and say, like the sirens in the second part of *Faust*: "Why do you dally / with this fabled horror?"

It is not easy to give a clear-cut answer to this question; the only thing one can do is to take refuge in that foolish dictum that there's no accounting for tastes, though the truth is that people scarcely do anything but try to account for them. The most usual method of dealing with the subject consists in referring to the well-stocked arsenal of psychoanalytical solutions, whose authority, in the perilous jungle of fear, seems indis-putable. According to the doctrine of Vienna, the source of our terrors is to be found in the guilt feelings hidden in the very depths of our psyche, the result of those early sexual conflicts which sweetened the faraway years of our childhood. Childish transgressions and impossible desires, with the consequent fear of mutilating punishment, have stamped our flesh with their mark of anxiety. The fear that goes back to the law transgressed before we were even able to formulate it besieges our dreams, converting them into nightmares. Some persons, particularly obsessed by that unforgettable sin which they cannot remem-ber, experience a certain joy—sadistic or masochistic? there must be a little of everything, for when the time comes to enjoy things we don't want to give up a single thrill—in seeing our most secret shudders literally represented; the invisible attacks that terrorize our souls are objectified and resolved on an im-aginary level. The monsters who wander through the darkness of which we consist at last consent to take on a face and form; though their actions may be frightening, at least the fact that they are throwing off their anonymity is something of a relief. Man learns to adore what tears at him for long enough; we live so long with the specter that bears our name that in the end we become quite fond of him. To give a certain bulk and coloration to the anguish that gnaws at us frees us from it in a certain sense by projecting it outward; but, more than anything else, it allows us to see it, that is, admire it. How can we not deeply respect, and even take pride in, that abominable shadow which is the only great thing that was in us!

This theory of the fascination that seems to be part of what frightens us may sound exceedingly paradoxical, all the more since it is essential to repeat that even admired anguish em-phatically does not cease to be anguish. But after all, the paradox contained in the psychoanalytical doctrine about dreams is no less of a paradox, despite all of Ernest Jones' rationalizing ef-forts. Even if we admit the compensatory and lenitive nature of dreams, whose purpose in large part is to maintain the state of sleep itself through the imaginary realization of desires that have gone unfulfilled during wakefulness, how can we explain the operation of nightmares, which sometimes prolong sleep as much as the happiest of dreams, but whose disagreeable and frightening traits appear to harmonize so little with the general doctrine about the role of our nighttime fantasies? The only way to make both positions agree is, I think, this: it must be admitted that to see and suffer through the complete story of our panic is one of the desires that disturb us, and the nightmare satisfies it with terrible generosity. Between sheets dripping with sweat and twisted by our convulsive movements, we experience a pleasure for which we pay a price so high that we cannot even recall it later as pleasure, once we are awake. But the bed, that damp and tumbled bed which seems to have undergone a storm of frantic love, gives us the lie.

I shall leave the psychoanalytical language to those who really know how to use it; that is, to those who still think in a more or less openly declared way that the problem is one of cure, or, more modestly, of correct diagnosis. I write from the viewpoint of nonknowledge, from never having learned that language, and above all from resistance to the idea of being cured—my problem is that I can't manage to get sufficiently worse, through lack of courage—and out of the almost-joyous confusion of the symptoms. First of all, we must emphasize the direct relationship of horror tales with death; the problem is death, its inevitability, its gloomy pomps, and, perhaps, its remedies. The subject of death leads us immediately to something that still has not been brought to light in this chapter, the supernatural character of the horror stories dealt with in it. Real fright, that fright which is always, either implicitly or explicitly, the fear of death, can have no other basis than the supernatural. Those who do not believe in the supernatural never tremble—stones, for instance, and some social insects. Among the higher animals it is not easy to find cases of such placidity. One need not understand the supernatural in the sense of the transcendent, the spiritual (?), or the magical, although it can eventually be expanded to those and other areas by extension. The supernatural is, simply, what is inadmissible from the viewpoint of necessity, what is unjustifiable by any form of legality, the spontaneity which, instead of joining the productive norm that reason establishes, violates itself like unreason. Death is, we are told, the absolutely necessary thing, the paradigm itself of the unavoidable. We, the future dead men, see it, however, as something shocking, like the flouting of all norms, like an awful or perverse function of the arbitrary. If we could regard death as something really necessary, as fully natural, nothing about it would strike us as terrifying—neither its presence nor the corruption that comes with it nor any of its symptoms. Everybody who has tried to purge us of the evils of death has recommended it as something natural and necessary (Spinoza, Hegel, common sense, science) or nonexistent (Epicurus and the Christians agree about this, for different reasons). The first excuse is negated by our intuition, the second by evidence. Death is not in the future but here and now, incessantly. Nothing is more false than to think it absent as long as we are here and to say that when it comes we will no longer be there to receive it. Death is not compatible with my present self but is its necessary foundation. But its necessity, its naturalness, which constitute precisely death's strength and what we most fear about it, are the aspects of death which frighten us most; that is what we cannot get used to. We pretend to a certain resigned acceptance, a hypocritical familiarity, but the procession of horror goes on inside us and peeps through the slightest chink in our rationalist armor. Fundamentally, what we like about the horror tale is the possibility of openly considering as supernatural that death to whose naturalness we are forced to give lip service daily.

But to admit that death is supernatural is to begin to cherish the forbidden hope of escaping from it. The unthinkable comes to the aid of the impossible. The proceedings that aspire to save us from annihilation pass through the most unbearable agonies. The general theory that underlies all these antideath aims is the one summed up in the verses of the German poet, which tell us that precisely where the danger lies in wait, there also grows what will free us from it, or, more simply, the well-known Latin tag *simil similibus curantur.* To shake off the shadow of death requires going down to death itself, entering the dreadful redoubt where it holds sway. "Death's lurking-place is worse than death itself," Seneca tells us. But there the funereal materials are found with which some will try to build a precarious immortality—the coffin filled with the vampire's native Balkan earth, the fragments of cadavers that compose the tormented body of the Promethean creature, the beams of moonlight that will perform the miracle of the werewolf, the terrifying mesmerism that keeps M. Valdemar's body from inevitable decomposition.

All naturalness lost, its false aspect as an obvious thing abandoned at last, death recovers its mantle of freezing mist or its disconsolate nocturnal howls; it joins hands with crime and the accursed but also with magic, with the incantation that brings bodies to life and the pact with the devil, which confers an ignominious vitality. The naturalistic concept of death tries to attenuate its presence, with methods that range from euphemistic expressions when speaking of it to the makeup applied to dead bodies (though this, on the other hand, is certainly an undeniable sign that it is not so easy to become accustomed to death's sway). The supernaturalism of terror, however, exacerbates death's presence to the point of intolerability, tears away the veils that hide its repellent nakedness, and emphasizes its gloomy charms as much as possible. This establishes a conflict between concealments and revelations. Instead of the neat funereal elimination of the mortal remains, which disappear in a trice, there is the spine-chilling account of confinement and asphyxiation whispered by the dead man, conscious of his entombment. Instead of the discreetly displayed photograph of the departed taken one day on the beach, and the gradual fading of his name from family conversations, there is a howling apparition of his ghost or the stink of putrefaction and disturbed earth that accompanies the revenant's footsteps. Instead of the sensible "Let's not think about it," imposed by common sense with regard to death, there is the morbid obsession of the necromantic, the nighttime frequenter of cemeteries, the dissector, or the man desperately in love with a dead woman's bloodless beauty. Instead of that sense of relief that goes along with realization of the inevitable, there is the mania for digging up, for putting together again, for resuscitating, for sending messages from the beyond, characteristic of all those people in tales of terror who cannot accept death. "Bad taste" is contrasted with good, with the ability to cover up death's ravages which defines the civilization based on it. The invisible world makes its claim, comes out in the open, makes us pay for hiding it with a noisy accentuation of its most alarming traits. Death loses all its distance from us and appears as it really is: lord and master, center of the world, the black smell of all existence, the necessary reference point of every action, every glance. But this unveiling of death works against it; death's undisguised appearance damages it. From its arrogance and stereotypes a new hope of life arises, an overwhelming fury that shakes and raises the dead man, extracting another, more lasting kind of vitality from what ought to have been permanent extinction. Cemeteries are filled with activity by night, ruins are again peopled with despairing inhabitants, new and unimaginable species grow in foul-smelling woods and swamps. Though in the end death succeeds in imposing its equilibrium, and dust returns to dust, the power of the absolutely necessary has been exposed for a moment to an intolerable exception; the suspicion slips in that an indomitable will can trick death, seeking its weapons in the slime of corruption itself.

There is more. Actually stating the horrible is subversive, within the bounds of a normality guaranteed by resignation to the deplorable—at least on the level of appearances. The tone itself of the horrifying story contains an attempt to refute death rather than expressing a morbid rejoicing in its triumph, as the superficial observer sometimes believes. It is indifference, however feigned and disguised as "maturity," which issues the death certificate, not the howl of terror. To grow accustomed to an evil means collaborating with it, no matter how many scientific reasons are brought forward for the need to be respectful of it. The tale of terror is based on proclaiming that the stroke of death's claws on reality is something we can never really get used to. But what ferocious changes take place in those who rebel against necessity! How high a price they pay for their subversive daring! Pale vampires with long fangs, ragged specters with cold curved claws, Lovecraft's abominable tentacular creatures, soulless puppets put together with cadavers, livid

virgins who return to consummate their impossible love, sor-
cerers who become more and more like the demons they keep
in their laboratory flasks. They are the unhappy heirs of the
Foremost Rebel, the tatters of flesh that the spirit leaves caught
on the barbed wire of reality when it tries to escape. Impaled,
burned, exorcised, scalded with dreaded holy water, they, the
protagonists of the horror story, are undoubtedly the true heroes of terrifying tales, and not those vapid, holier-than-thou
creatures who prevail over them at the end of the story. Their
name is Legion—the legion of the wounded in the greatest of
wars of independence, of the revolution against death. Despite
their inevitable final defeat, their mere attempt already constitutes a victory. The reader's feelings toward them are delicately
ambiguous, resembling a terrorized recognition, a sort of
frightened sympathy. On the one hand our peace of mind, our
order, and our sanity demand that they be destroyed, that the
menace they represent be smashed; but on the other hand we
inevitably identify with their desires, and in our heart of hearts
discover that their desperate howls are our secret hymn. They
are the greatest danger that awaits us but also one of our best
possibilities. Maybe we do not share their decision to seek arms
against death in death itself, which presupposes, after all, a
certain inverted recognition of its necessity and a new and hopeless justification of the inexorable; but in any case their struggle
brings them closer to us, or at least brings them closer to the
least submissive part of us. Despite our horror, their exploits
are the ones that interest us and not the exploits of those who
finish them off or escape from their clutches. What attracts us
to them is an open secret, which can be expressed in these terms:
we are of the same stock as ghosts.

   Are we not, perchance, as supernatural as they, no matter
how hard we try to bring ourselves down to the level of a
"naturalness" which every one of our actions, not to mention
our thoughts, denies with the innermost strength of conviction?
The abominable strangeness of monsters' bodies duplicates the
alarmed astonishment we feel about our own. We too have
tentacles and fetid excretions and undergo changes we cannot
control, and are gradually becoming something that is totally

alien to us and that will end by terrifying us. They have hastened the process, that is all; they have felt an impatience to go right to the end, to try to go further still, to try to use degradation to their advantage. We recognize ourselves in their busy quiverings, in that insatiable soul which perverts life by trying to intensify it, in that fundamental, unmixed solitude of the inescapably different. If I'm pushed a little I will even say that monsters offer us the reverse of saintliness, owing no less to the sacred simply because it is black. The ghosts of horror stories are the blessed ones of that mad god who appeared to Lovecraft, howling in the darkness; his blood-curdling hagiography is both disconsolate and unconsoling, but it wounds us in our most vulnerable spot.

I have made a direct connection between the tale of terror and the supernatural; someone will be sure to remind me of the statement by Jacques Bergier, who makes Lovecraft "the inventor of the materialist terror tale." I think that I have made sufficiently clear what I understand by *supernatural* to be able to state that if *materialist* means something like "what is determined by necessary physical laws," the French critic's judgment is totally erroneous. Lovecraft's stories, like those of Machen, Chambers, and Hope Hodgson, are just as supernatural—in the sense I mentioned before—as any classical nineteenth-century ghost story, though it is true that they moved the challenge to necessity out of the space in which their predecessors had placed it. Before, the elements that sustained the inexorable were of a Christian and religious kind and served as a framework for the excursions of specters and vampires, still debtors to the devil and enemies of the Cross. Later, necessity assumed a scientific face, and the rebellion against it began to present itself as extravagances of archaeology, physics, or medicine, but this was true quite a long time before Lovecraft. It is true of Mary Wollstonecraft Shelley's famous novel and of *The Facts in the Case of M. Valdemar*. What has changed has been the concept of the natural, which before was subject to the designs of providence and today is subject to those of science. Terror tales continue to appeal to the supernatural, whether this be the diabolical aspects of the Christian faith or the points at which scientific knowledge encounters a terrifying limit that breaks down its concept of normality.

In this regard, it is curious to point out the large part played by a certain type of neopaganism in the works of Machen, Blackwood, and Lovecraft. The term *paganism* must be taken in its most literal sense, for in most cases it is a question of forbidden cults that survive in forgotten villages, remote from urban, industrial civilization. In the devil-worship of the classical warlocks and vampires, or Lewis' accursed monk, pulsed the irrepressible presence of the much-persecuted Manichaean dualism, Christianity's old twin brother. In Lovecraft's beings of the Old Order, or in Blackwood's elemental spirits, the outlawed pluralities of polytheism reclaim their rights. Monotheism, both the Christian kind and the science-oriented kind, continues to place terror in that difference and diversity which are opposed to it and looks with horror on the distinct return of the unforeseeable in the realm of the inevitably foreseeable, the return of the most terrifyingly remote past, which comes to disturb the dogma of progress with its poisoned emanations. The root of the panic lies in the fact that great Pan is not dead.

To sit down next to the fireplace and start to read a perfect story by Montague Rhodes James, or to squeeze into the subway as you read in snatches the magical lines of the wonderful Jean Ray—tombs yawn, ghosts emerge, and suspicious heaps of rags crawl along the sidewalk after us, or Number 13 of any street can be Maupertuis. The die is cast. We are victims of the oldest vice that literature has propagated—the desire for horrifying tales. Both good taste and every literary precept forbid us; psychiatry places us among the obsessive neurotics or mental defectives and recommends cold showers; the advocate of educational and politically conscious literature deplores the puerility of our escape mechanism. But we take no notice of anyone but Sade, only Sade, when he whispers in our ears, "Extinguish your soul, try to turn everything that alarms your heart into enjoyment."

# 13

## THE MURDERER WHO
## LEAVES NO CLUES

I have hitherto confined my investigations to this world," said
he. "In a modest way I have combated evil, but to take on the
Father of Evil himself would, perhaps, be too ambitious a task.
Yet you must admit that the footmark is material."

Sir Arthur Conan Doyle, *The Hound of the Baskervilles*

I HAVE JUST FINISHED reading an excellent detective novel, *There Came Both Mist and Snow*. For some time now I have been a devotee of its author, Michael Innes, whose *Hamlet, Revenge!* I consider one of the best-written books of the genre.[1] In *There Came Both Mist and Snow* he performs a tour de force which endangers the very existence of this type of story: each of the characters is in turn declared guilty, all the solutions are possible, but none is correct. Intelligent virtuosity is carried so far that the reader closes the book in exasperation, with a certain prickle of dissatisfaction. On the one hand he has savored the excitement of heightened imagination to the point of depravity; on the other, he has turned round and round in a void, and in view of the final result, the whole effort seems superfluous, futile. This state of mind, from which I have so often suffered when I finish the reading of philosophy, inspires me to compare these two literary genres—the detective story and speculative narration.

It is obvious that philosophy is a literary genre, characterized by the recurrence of certain modes of expression and certain themes. Some people will smile with satisfaction as they read this statement, which they will perhaps think damaging to a philosopher. Philosophy recognizes that it is literature, fiction, a whim of imagination; the person who wants to obtain true knowledge must either resort to science or ask the realm of public affairs for a formula. These simpletons do not know that literature is anything but whimsical, and that the idea of "real knowledge" is in fact an invention of philosophy and has no meaning outside philosophical discourse. Philosophy is not narration, and therefore it renounces true truth; it is a narration whose plot is the search for truth. In the course of that search the meaning of the concept of "truth" is established, and hence it would be absurd to say that the truth is not in philosophy but in science, politics, or religion, given the fact that to determine *where* truth lies is precisely philosophy's task. But all this has been said before, in many other places. What I want to establish is this: philosophy is a form of narration; speculation is the development of a plot, in the discursive as well as the dramatic meaning of the term.

Along general lines it can be said that the novel is a literary genre notable for the plasticity of its forms and the laxness of the conventions that constitute it. Roger Caillois, in *Puissances du roman*, expounds on this point with a degree of accuracy not achieved, in my opinion, by his book as a whole.[2] The detective story, however, has an extremely rigid structure. Even without admitting all the rules that the members of the Detection Club swore to observe and according to which they wrote *The Floating Admiral*,[3] it would not be impossible to draw up, with a certain degree of precision, a list of laws whose infraction (except in the case of a genius) would spoil this kind of story and disappoint its enthusiasts. The ingenious exceptions based on a clever flouting of the norm (as in the so-often copied example of the narrator-murderer in Agatha Christie's *The Murder of Roger Ackroyd*), rely for their effect on the reader's implicit acceptance of this unwritten code.

Well, all this can also be said of that type of narration called philosophy. In both cases there is an attempt to bring out into the open the internal logic of apparently unconnected events; in both cases we are dealing with a search which strings together one deduction after another until final truth is attained, in the light of which the whole story takes on its final meaning and is simultaneously made superfluous. Once one has fully understood either a detective story or a philosophical system, one's long progress toward the light becomes unbearable, impossible to read again. Obviously both genres assume the responsibility of offering an outcome that will make everything clear; a confession of total ignorance at the end of a detective story or a treatise on metaphysics would be viewed as an intolerable fraud. In philosophy as in criminal fiction, the discovery of truth immediately carries with it a moral posture, the adoption of a more or less clearly defined distinction between evil and good, between the villain and the good people or between the good person and the villains (the detective story tends toward the first of these by isolating the criminal in his sinister singularity, while philosophy inclines toward the second by beatifying the righteous man in contrast to the malign majority; we need not recall the case of Socrates).

The two genres share an identical aversion to the useless

detail; there are no allowable digressions, everything has to agree with, point toward, or refer to the final truth. If in a detective story a cup is described slowly and deliberately, it can only be for two justifiable reasons; either knowledge of that cup helps to cast light on the crime, or it is a false clue intended to thicken the plot. In this case, any touch of literary whim would infuriate the true devotee. And in the same way, in a properly constructed speculative theory, it would be intolerable to introduce an excursus that would not agree with the general principle of the system, unless it described one of the difficulties encountered in the elucidation of that principle. Both genres exclude the gratuitous, the inexplicable, whatever is irreducible to the definitive solution on the final pages—exact and strict limits which disdain any appeal to chance. On the other hand, both the criminal writer and the philosopher make it a point of honor to keep feeding the reader all the clues concerning the development of the matter in such a way that an ideal enthusiast of the genre, aided only by logic, could complete for himself the elucidation of the criminal's identity or the whole scope of the philosophical system. But in fact both kinds of authors manage to obscure so diabolically the matter they are trying to explain that they usually make it imperative to read the book to the very end. Another resemblance: no matter how great an effort is made to avoid it, in philosophy as in criminology, loose ends always remain, which often obsess the reader after he has closed the book, though he ought to be happy now that he knows the really important part of it.

Both the philosopher and the detective are seeking the solution to an enigma, broken down into a few elementary questions. Why? Who? How? In the case of the philosopher the *mysterium magnum* embraces the entire universe; apparently more modest but resembling him in essentials, the detective seeks the identity of the performer of an action. Does not knowing unequivocally the cause of a single thing imply discovering that of all things? It is a question of knowing who is responsible, who is hiding behind appearances, concealed and revealed by them in equal measure. There must be awareness of everything that has happened, either in the cosmos or the room where the crime took place. No less in one case than the other, the heart of the matter lies in applying strictly the principle of sufficient reason: everything has a cause, a foundation, an intention; nothing happens "just because." A disgraceful event—a crime or the suspicion of one—disturbs the seamless solidity of a certain order of things; it must be restored, repaired, and each piece must be returned to its place. To do so, reality must be reinvented, the path that has led each thing to its present place must be retraced. It is a desperate task, perhaps, for no one can revive the victim to find out who his murderer was, nor can the wound of thought be entirely healed by the balm of a completed system. The crime writer's undertaking, like the philosopher's, consists in a sort of detached acceptance which in the end is useless. Both attempts at dispassionateness, if they are not to be tedious, soulless charades, need the abysmal presence of death. They take from it their importance, their urgency, their more or less justified touch of impassioned grandeur. A detective story without death, or the threat of it, is only a silly hieroglyph, as vacuously conventional as a crossword puzzle, exactly the same as a philosophical system that avoids or plays down the subject of death, prey to more "scientific" questions or more positive treatments. Anglo-Saxons do not usually commit the first of these errors, but they succumb to the second with astounding frequency, and so they are much more to be trusted as detective-story writers than as philosophers.

There is another point—the reader has already guessed it— on which philosophy and the detective story resemble each other: both are endangered species, at least in their classical form. Neither the great philosophical systems nor the great detectives have a future; over-ingenious explanations are not trusted. Sociology threatens to devour both these narrative styles, whose traditional models crumble under the combined attack of brutality and obscenity, when not of political denunciation. There is no doubt that both violence and questions about its origin will continue to be essential literary motifs. It is no less certain that the stylistic conventions which until now have ruled the setting forth of both kinds of plot—which are fundamentally the same, as I have already hinted—are in process of disappearing. Lovers of the old style will undoubtedly suffer in the transition; that is, if they manage to get completely used to novelty and do not choose to develop ostentatious antiquarian tastes. In *Murder off Miami*, by Wheatley and Links, the traditional book form has been replaced by a folder containing police reports, photographs, fingerprints, and pieces of bloodstained cloth. Reading is replaced by the jigsaw puzzle; the narrator is barely present; the courteous exercise of listening to the story in the order preferred by someone else is no longer necessary. Positivistic scientism has no less effectively dismembered speculative writing, now separated into isolated data, logico-mathematical formulas, and production curves. In both cases there is the same haste to lay hands on something, to manipulate it. It is no longer a question of relating the development of a meaning, but of proffering a handful of instruments. But the truth thus obtained inevitably becomes trivial, and what is worse, it does so without becoming more modest or more skeptical with respect to its quality as final truth. Does this bring us closer to a decisive awakening of our ancestral terrors? or does the personalization of fear multiply their sting? We are progressing toward criminals without a name, words without an origin, communities without a basis. If only a faultless new Sherlock Holmes would also flourish in that wasteland and, like his namesake, halt in time the diabolical hound who seeks our blood!

In August 1975 an important minor news event quietly stirred the summer somnolence of the press. Agatha Christie had decided to publish her novel *Curtain*, written many years earlier, in which she killed off her famous and dandified Hercule Poirot. Those nostalgic for the good old days, and all idle folk, shuddered in their sun-drenched lounge chairs at the thought of this new affront by the grandmother of crime. The newspapers gave generous space to the matter, probably in gratitude to the English writer and her unexpected gift of this news—freely offered, but with a slight touch of humor and the macabre. I was asked for a few pages on the subject, and this is what I wrote, more or less:[4]

Betrayal (involuntary betrayal, according to the legend) by the woman who loved him most was the cause of Hercules' death, seared by his bloody tunic. Now another Hercules has died, also betrayed by the woman who should love him best. Someone will say that, after all, Dame Agatha is the owner of her character: she gave him to us, she takes him away. A grave error. Poirot is not a gift that can be snatched away from us: he is the dream not of one person but of many. Perhaps this is precisely what has motivated his mother-in-law's—I mean his mother-in-literature's—criminal jealousy: Dame Agatha has caught on to the fact that Poirot had left her to go off with someone else, with anybody, with everybody. She was merely one of many; her Belgian may have whispered "je t'aime" to her at night in his ridiculous language-course accent (and badly learned at that), but she probably answered peevishly, "I'll bet you say that to all the girls." From this jealous viewpoint, she had plenty of reasons to work up a grudge against him. And it must not be at all comfortable to have that lady as an enemy, if we consider that she has one of the longest criminal records in Europe. She is Locusta in a cottage, a more hypocritical and tea-loving Elizabeth Bathory.

I am sure that she has planned her crime long and carefully. At eighty-five, the paroxysm of passion must be dismissed. And anyway, it isn't Dame Agatha's style, for she is a niggling perfectionist with more twists than an old-fashioned corkscrew. No indeed, we can be certain of premeditation. And also trickery, as in *The Murder of Roger Ackroyd*, when the unsuspecting reader heard the impersonal voice of a narrator whom he took to be good old Hastings, only to find that it was that of the murderer himself. Mrs. Christie must have chosen the time and place with maniacal care, must have prepared the most reliable weapon, must have provided herself with an ironclad alibi.

And anyway, who is going to unmask her now that *he* is gone?

But if I were in your shoes, dear lady, I would not be too confident. No crime is easy (with the possible exception of those committed on a grand scale and in the service of noble ideals), but those involving great detectives entail special risks. There is the case of Conan Doyle, who also decided one day that there would be a "final problem" for the greatest of the great, for Sherlock Holmes. He found him a tremendous adversary—an Antichrist—and carried him off to Switzerland (Holmes, who traveled so seldom despite his mythical middle-European missions in aid of threatened monarchies!) and threw him off a raging waterfall, locked in mortal embrace with his archcriminal Moriarty. It was all in vain. Indignant letters from clients and friends of the Baker Street detective poured in on Sir Arthur; some of them addressed him as a "great brute" and went on from there. Even the novelist's aged mother had been totally won over by that clever grandson of hers, a morphine addict and violinist, and interceded for him with her son. Conan Doyle made an attempt to recount another case of Holmes' without bothering to resuscitate him, as if it were a posthumous adventure: and so he confronted him with the ominous night on the wastes of Dartmoor, assailed by a supernatural hound. But the public didn't want Holmes to be dead; what is more, they *knew* that he wasn't. Death, Dame Agatha, is neither fair nor necessary. Those clichés about "all of us have to go through it" or "it's the law of life" are solemn stupidities. Only the victims of boredom, enmity, hard work, exploitation, merely die: all the rest of us die by murder. That is why we like detective stories, where no death goes unpunished and all deaths reveal behind them, no matter how "natural" they appear to be, a wicked, destructive design which the great detective will undertake to uncover and punish. Well, I should hope so! Death has no power over the hero: it is enough to be Sherlock Holmes, D'Artagnan, Hercule Poirot, or Flash Gordon, never to

die. That is what we are seeking when we read their adventures, a *life* forever threatened and forever triumphant,
the defeat of the necessity of death. Sancho Panza was
right when he reproached Don Quixote for being so determined to die: "Do not die, your worship, my master,
but take my advice and live many years; for the most
foolish thing a man can do in this life is to let himself die
without rhyme or reason, without anybody killing him,
or any hands but those of melancholy making an end of
him." Good for Sancho! Dying was a betrayal that Alonso
Quijano tried to perpetrate on the Knight of the Woeful
Countenance, but fortunately he failed utterly. Just as happened with the attempt to kill Sherlock Holmes or as,
probably, will happen with your attempt, Dame Agatha,
to finish off the absurd and delightful Poirot.

Sherlock Holmes lives in London, not far from Trafalgar
Square, in a small room above the pleasant commotion
of a pub that bears his name and which has been made into
a museum of his adventures. I went to see him not long
ago: there were his pipe, his violin, the dummy murdered
by a bullet on one dangerous occasion. While I was there
a troop of Americans noisily climbed the stairs leading to
Holmes' little room; a fat lady asked me, "Where is he?"
and I answered, "He has gone out to take a turn around
Whitechapel, madam, but he may return at any moment."
And it was the literal truth.[5]

That is why I feel obliged to warn you very seriously,
Mrs. Christie, about the risks you will run by trying to
liquidate Poirot. I know that by killing him you are attempting to show that you are still the boss, and we'll go
along with you as far as that. But don't be careless. You
think that Hercule Poirot is a character you created; but
if you really think about it, isn't the opposite more likely?
As far as we know Agatha Christie is an old lady with
neatly combed hair whose picture appears on the dust
jackets of Poirot's novels. They say that you are married
to an archaeologist and that you like to play bridge. People
like that turn up only in Poirot's cases. Forgive me, but

really you are quite unbelievable. Suspicious, very suspicious! I believe that Agatha Christie is an invention of Poirot's, so that he can tell about his cases without sinning too much on the side of vanity and yet without ceasing to praise himself as often as possible. Try to kill him, madam, and you will see what happens: your picture will gradually disappear from dust jackets and you will have completely ceased to exist. Remember, there is no such thing as a perfect crime.

The last paragraph of my article was fully confirmed, for Agatha Christie did not survive even by six months the execution of her literary character. Comparatively speaking, her death went more unnoticed than Poirot's. No one was deceived about which of them was authentically *real* and which a mere character in a book. At any rate, I am no longer so sure about the real culprit in Poirot's murder. François de Lyonnais, in an interesting presentation of the structures of the detective story, reaches the conclusion that the only solution that has never been offered in the genre is the one in which it would turn out that the criminal is the reader himself.[6] Perhaps this denouement has not been used precisely because the hypocritical reader is always the fellow creature and brother of the criminal, the detective, and even the victim—an embarrassing plurality of roles. Now, in the case of Poirot's death, I would not be surprised if in the end the murderer turned out to be either the reader himself or a proliferating hydra-headed monster: the readers. Affected, absurdly pretentious, slightly ridiculous but no more or less so than the artificial English world he inhabits, Poirot must have realized that he was increasingly losing the esteem of readers inclined toward action and cybernetics. Mrs. Christie's political confusion, which led her to juxtapose a resuscitated Hitler with "hippies" and other young folk of bad living habits, must not have contributed to his survival either. Since he does not possess Sherlock Holmes' strong poetic aura, Poirot's resurrection is for the moment doubtful, though it cannot be dismissed entirely. After all, in case of death, who doesn't more or less expect to rise again?[7]

I am a rather old-fashioned fan when it comes to detective stories (and probably when it comes to everything else). I like the apparently calm air of expectation that precedes the crime, the sudden series of bodies, the locked rooms, the impossible situations verging on the supernatural, the ingenious solutions, and the delicious disillusionment when explanations are made. I don't care much for the "tough" novel, which tends to bore me even in its most eminent representatives, Raymond Chandler and Chester Himes. It is a genre I consider much more appropriate to the movies than to the novel. The blonde, alcoholic, perverted girls, the cynical but generous detectives, the unpleasant police inspectors, and the fat, cruel gangsters do not wear well in the reading but are an unsurpassed triumph in the hands of a John Huston or a Jean-Pierre Melville. At least, this is my opinion. Maybe I have never loved any character in fiction as much as Sherlock Holmes. I don't know exactly what the secret is that places him so far above the others of his ilk. I suppose it has something to do with his belonging to that early moment in the science of detection when it was still romantic and personal and also with a certain spare but sparkling style of heroism and readiness for adventure of which the hermit of Baker Street was an unforgettable incarnation. In any case, the mystery of his magnetism remains intact. After the work of Conan Doyle, the crime novels I prefer—and with them I bring this general confession to a close—are those of John Dickson Carr, who sometimes writes as Carter Dickson. *The Burning Court* and *The Unicorn Murders* recount impossible and extremely vivid happenings with gloomy, ghostlike shadows overhanging them, resolved in the end with elegant logic. He is a very able storyteller with a macabre and very appealing sense of humor.

The first detective case in literature was solved, as is well known, by the prophet Daniel. Confronted by the idolatrous priests of Baal, who insisted that the god ate the food that was offered to him daily, he invented a perfect system for unmasking his adversaries. During the night he sprinkled ashes around the god's altar where the offerings were placed and next day found on the blackened floor the marks of human footsteps, which accused Baal's worshippers of fraud, pious thieves of the food the god was supposed to devour miraculously. Centuries later, Sherlock Holmes found the enormous tracks of a supernatural dog which for generations had haunted the Baskervilles and, though not without giving the devil some credit, insisted that those footmarks were real. As Daniel also knew, neither gods nor ghosts leave a mark where they step.

## ADDENDUM

Detractors, defenders, and theoreticians of the detective story have darkened a great many sheets of paper in the last forty or fifty years. There has been an abundance of triteness, no lack of ingeniousness and profundity; but perhaps the only really interesting thing has been arrant nonsense. This latter category has an undeniably remarkable representative in Dr. Roldán Cortés, the convicted and self-confessed author of a little book bearing the vibrant title *Influencia de la literatura moderna en las enfermedades mentales*, with the inevitable preface by Don Gregorio Marañón. Either Don Gregorio was unable to resist turning out yet another little preface or he must have owed the author a large personal favor. The book raves on, with enviable vigor, about topics as different as literary mysticism, anarchist literature, eroticism, realism, and even "detailism" (?), this last a genre "very much in vogue in our day," as we are told (the book was perpetrated in 1940, as its content makes obvious). The author does a thorough job on "detectivism," as he calls it; I can't resist extracting some especially delicious passages from his diatribe.

The narrators of these episodes à la Conan Doyle have against them the absence of all moral intention and the unbridled desire to turn the feeble brains for whom they write into complicated mazes. By piling up scenes of dramatic plot complications, that is, like perverted music-hall turns, they overemphasize and press down on the minor spring of curiosity, which is so well developed in uncultivated imaginations, with all sorts of clever tricks. In all these novels, unlike those of the century that produced the novels of chivalry, shines a spirit of feminine wilinesss mixed with an atmosphere of criminal cynicism. We find no huge, virile adventures, no knightly challenges. Gadgets and pretense, ambushes and attacks, robbery and masquerades. This is the content of such productions.

Many psychic dangers lie in wait for those unfortunates who enter such a treacherous swamp. On the one hand Dr. Roldán Cortés reminds us of the recognized risk of emotional identification with the criminal, followed logically enough by "the irresistible desire to emulate his exploits, neither more nor less than in the sadly Spanish days of the notorious bandits Diego Corrientes, the Candelas brothers, or the Seven Lads of Ecija." But still more serious, if that is possible, will be the unbalancing of

imaginations which consider themselves to be on a higher plane and which, for this reason, have some glimmering of morals; they lose themselves in such reading, identify with the inflexible duty represented, in this case, by the police, and on occasion carry their obsession to such an extreme that, believing they are Sherlock Holmes, they try to apply detection to the reality of life itself, and even suffer from a genuine persecution mania with respect to their friends, their acquaintances, even their family.

There can be no doubt that this hyper-policemanly behavior is frequently detestable and takes us back to other, alas! no less sadly Spanish days than those of the large-spirited Andalusian bandits but much closer to our own time.

To summarize, I need only subscribe to Marañón's opinion of Dr. Roldán Cortés in his prologue: "I could say nothing, for myself, about this small and very attractive book, except merely that I like it very much."

# 14

## BORGES:
## DOUBLE VERSUS SINGLE

It is I, it is Borges. . . .

Jorge Luis Borges, "The Aleph"
*The Aleph and Other Stories, 1933–1969*

ALL WRITERS HAVE SECRETS; if they hadn't, what would they write about? Secret sorrows, secret deficiencies, secret ambitions, secret concupiscience, secret disorders. The fundamental thing about Borges is the primarily *literary* nature of all his secrets. Nothing is so surprising as to find, at last, someone really possessed by literature, someone who obtains all his points of reference from it and owes it all his contents. Borges, a man possessed by poetry, bewitched by tales and stories. It is here that Borges' special, moving limpidity resides—no extra-literary secret, but all the unencompassable vastness of literature as secret. Limpidity: Borges has slowly constructed a bright challenge to the shadows, whose transparency has all the attributes of something veiled and the ominous palpitation of darkness. It is not a twilight, brilliant but on the point of being devoured by shadows, like Proust's; it is a blazingly es-oteric noon, whose light blinds us like the profoundest of mysteries because it is the profoundest mystery. As E. M. Cioran tells us, "Authentic vertigo is the absence of madness." No

writer is more uncompromisingly sane than Borges, or more vertiginous.

It is a hard-won sanity, which demands a whole complex ritual in order to maintain itself. That is why Borges' poetry and prose are so rich in those repetitions of subjects and modes which possess a highly ceremonial character, in the consolidation of the cosmos through its renovation. Borges the ceremonious, the pagan high priest. Satisfactory celebration of the rite demands a privileged and naked kind of readiness, a memory zealous of its limits, a sacredly ordering will which draws strength from the implacable contemplation of the dreadful fragility of all order, the vision of chaos. That ceremonial vocation can seem mannered if it is considered from a desacralizing standpoint; that is, from an ingenuously optimistic view of reality. The demythification of the world, the trivialization of each of its aspects—"it's only . . ."—does not presuppose so much its liberation from the oppression of the sacred as its total surrender to the necessity of law, a necessity institutionalized in the significant expression "natural laws." Hence nutrition or sexuality lose all their mystery and are reduced to organic processes, the movement of the stars or the movement of rivers to physical processes, the composition of bodies to chemical formulas. Behind each mystery that has been eliminated appears a necessary law; having escaped from the arbitrariness of the aleatory, behold us subjugated to the necessary. The total profanation of the world is accomplished by its total ordering, by its transformation into a manipulable object, in accordance with the law of its nature, which has the dual function of authorizing its use by wiping out the sacred aura which infused respect and at the same time showing how to perform that manipulation. This concept is optimistic because it does away with chaos once and for all (chaos, which was only ignorance of the law), but only ingenuously or superficially, for it exchanges uncertainty—freedom, in the last instance—for the iron disenchantment of necessity. In any case, ritual ceremonies lose their meaning, whose expression was myth, for they can only take shape with chaos as their background and constant reference; the law makes them inexplicable, that is, useless. The stronger the law is, the less relevance do ceremonies and rites have, and they become affected, ridiculous, and superstitious acts.

In literature this superstitious artificiality is called mannerism, and from the point of view I have described nothing seems more logical than to apply the label to the ceremonious Borges. But, while in the world of the law the only sanity consists in more or less enlightened submission, the unequivocal presence of chaos turns sanity into an improbable adventure and makes necessary a careful interpretation of freedom itself. Such an interpretation of freedom (in the dual sense of "laying bare" and "representing") is carried out in rites and their corresponding myths. For good or ill (for good and ill), Borges' sanity has been *won*, not merely accepted. This consideration casts a decisive light on Borges' conservatism—in all its manifestations—which, contrary to the opinion of the scandalized progressivists who admire him, is not superficial whim but a perfectly lucid consequence of his deepest thought.

His confinement within literature does not place Borges at a distance from that confusing abstraction "reality." On the contrary, it places him in the heart of reality, or better still in the reality of reality. The fact that he has realized that discourse is the reality of reality makes Borges the most modern of authors, that is, the one who has taken best advantage of having appeared later than the rest. To be sure, this nuclearly *real* condition of literature has not been fully revealed until quite recently, and it makes Borges' writing possible. By "literary" must be understood not only that which is usually considered narration or poetry, but also those other poetic forms or narratives which are philosophy, theology, scientific theory, political constitutions, or revolutionary proclamations. It is absolutely obtuse to continue to insist on the fictitious and invented nature of the literary, in contrast to the condition of being real and given which the hypothetical real world is supposed to possess. The literary is precisely what is really given us at every moment, what morally conditions our actions, what explains to us scientifically the "truth" of everything around us, everything that creates our identity and a name of our own, the thing that gives form to our amorous transports or our political urgencies. The very distinction between words and things, between theory and practice, between literature and real world, is wholly literary. Inventions and imaginings begin precisely when we try to take over the "natural" or to return to the primacy of "real life"; for, unable to abandon the literary orbit, we keep on making worse literature, vaguer and more divagatory, fuller of recourse to the "ineffable" or to desperately abstract terms such as "there," "this," "now." Perhaps in some faraway time things were not as bad as this, though we can hardly imagine it, and certainly the world has always ingenuously believed that it understood existence in a different way (I say "has *believed*" because it has never been able to actually *think* it); but starting with Hegel, Nietzsche, or Saussure things must have been pretty clear. What happens is that Borges has been particularly unable to maintain the conventional literary distinction between discourse about the world and the world itself, which on a certain plane—the one Hegel called the plane of *understanding*—is indispensable for the normal functioning of the State, and this has placed his writing on a level so implacably realistic that common sense (namely, the interiorization of the law) can no longer view it as such and consigns it to the genre of fantasy or escapism. All of Borges' controlled emotionalism resides, simply, in his declared inability to catch the other tiger, "the one that is not in the verse"; but this inability is not a proof of inevitable escapism into the fabulous but of his realism, because that tiger which is not in the verse does not exist.

Literature as the only secret: this is the key to Borges' work. Superficially, this key is demonstrated by the constant presence of literary objects in his pages—books, libraries, quotations, more or less apocryphal scholarly references, commentaries on famous works of literature, the recreation of classic themes, variations on these, discussions between writers or theologians, and so on. At each turn of the page, a new appearance of his primary myth: the blind man, with the double blindness that prevents him from seeing the "real" world—from catching the tiger that is not in the verse—and reading books, walking through the endless library in which are written dawns, pyramids, and gardens, or perhaps strolling—he does not know this, for he is blind—among dawns, pyramids, and gardens, which are the symbols God's book is written in. The blind man's indifference to either of these two viewpoints, his total inability finally to settle the dispute between them, in some sense makes them equal, makes them identical. One must be blind to appearances, given over only to memory, to discover the essential irrelevance of the distinction between discourse and life, which on practical levels seems overwhelmingly important.

In memory both tigers are identical, indistinguishable, for there has never been more than one. Kant let slip a dangerous suspicion when he revealed that a hundred dreamed-about talers are no more and no less real than a hundred actual ones. If they are equally real, the very distinction between what is dreamed and what is actual becomes more and more problematical. With this Kant thought he had demolished the ontological argument, but what he really did was reinforce it; for what St. Anselm actually said was that God is, in any sense, the real par excellence, even though he is only a dreamed-about God. The guardian of the library is either blind or does not know how to read, which for Borges is the same thing, and because of this, forced to depend on memory, he has discovered the radical identity between signifier and signified, the literary essence of the world. But this knowledge sets him apart from other men, prevents him from enjoying books and other things, confines him within the only activity that is possible for him, remembering. The erudition, the quotations, the ideal picture, are not an option among others but the only one that remains to him—that or silence. There is no writing that is less innocent, less direct; but full acceptance of every text's character as a palimpsest, his withdrawal from all intermediate deceptions—so-called realism, psychologism, subjective confession—endow Borges with a seductive primitivism; and he, who writes as we know certainly that nobody could have written at the beginning, sometimes seems to be the primordial writer.

But literature as the only secret appears—or better still, hides—at a deeper level than that of the presence of literary objects in his texts. The fabric itself of Borges' work has only one central motif, inexhaustibly repeated: duplication. Borges' essential duplicity. Literature is the real world's double and eventually takes its place so that we can no longer know if there once was such a thing as a "world" outside literary creation. An endless literary game of duplications: word and object, form and content, signifier and signified, plot and style, author and characters, invention and observation, ethics and aesthetics, fiction and reportage. Each of these terms seems to be defined in relation to the other, which is contrasted with it; a deeper examination reveals that all the attributes of one correspond to the other, with a change of level and a difference in emphasis. We observe that there are two superimposed, parallel worlds, which memory (or that specialized type of memory, thought) makes into one. To read or to live; the tiger who is sung about and the one that is not in the verse. Borges' only theme is this dual composition of the world, precisely because his only secret is literature, or, better still, his secret and literature's are the same. All of Borges can be summarized in the title of one of his books: the other, the same. His two favorite philosophers— apart, naturally, from Plato, the duplicator par excellence—are those who have based their systems on a duplicity reconciled, in the last instance, with the one: thus Spinoza, whose single substance does not consent to reveal to us more than two of its infinite attributes, thought and extension, and Schopenhauer, in whose system the world is composed of will and representation. They are the two philosophers whose thought must most inevitably be understood as a *reading* of the universe. And it would not be hard to find an identical motif in the storytellers Borges loves most dearly: in Poe, who told the story of a man supplanted and finally killed by his double; in Stevenson, who wove the terrible adventure of the scientist split into two morally opposed persons; in Chesterton, who glimpsed the deeply powerful identity between the Prince of Order and the Prince of Anarchy. The theme appears in Borges' work under all its forms and in all its shadings. Fundamentally, we can say that the principle of duplication is accomplished in Borges through the recurrence of three ceremonies, whose constant repetition is not free of crossings and recrossings. We shall call them the ceremony of the Mirror, the ceremony of the Labyrinth, and the ceremony of the *Imago mundi*. We shall say a word about each of them, with no exhaustive intent that goes beyond the merely indicative character of this note.

The ceremony of the Mirror renews the most directly accessible form of duplication. One element recognizes itself in the other as being the same; like seeks its like, between symmetry and difference, just as Alice finds, through the looking-glass, an identical but reversed world. Mirrors condemned by the heresiarchs of Tlön because their reproductive function resembled that of paternity, no less repudiated by them. Symmetry of the other side of the world, beyond death, where Poe continues to weave terrible portents and Baltasar Gracián busies himself with niggling trifles. The other Borges, who is little by little taking over Borges and who writes what are perhaps his best pages; or that young self whom Borges finds seated on a bench beside a river that flows simultaneously in the United States and Switzerland. It is history repeated with an elusive and marvelous vacillation—the knives that renew their duel in other hands after their masters are dead: the improvised evangelist who repeats the events of the Gospels and finds himself condemned to the cross like Christ; God looking at a rabbi, His creature, with discouragement identical to that with which the rabbi looks at the golem he has made; or the sorcerer of the circular ruins, who has dreamed a man and knows in the end that he himself is dreamed—or Borges following Groussac's very tracks and repeating his blindness surrounded by books. It is the tiger who is sung about and the one not in the verse, the transcendent tiger of fearful symmetry. Or it is identification in the work, the length and breadth of space and the centuries: FitzGerald recreating *The Rubáiyat* of the epicurean Persian, Pierre Ménard modestly repeating the *Quixote*, or any one of us being a new Shakespeare by repeating Hamlet's soliloquy. There is a higher duplication in creation: the duplication that Shakespeare himself experienced after his death, when he met his maker and learned that He also was everyone and no one, as Shakespeare was with respect to his characters. Sometimes the mirror ends by equalizing what was put forward as an unresolvable opposition, as in the case of those two theologians who believed that they were implacable rivals and later learned that in God's eyes they were only one. There is also the case of the reproduction so ambitious that it aspires to take the place of its model, like that map whose size and great detail made it different in no detail from the land that it mapped. But the great ceremony of the Mirror is, without a doubt, Funes of the remarkable memory, with his tireless mnemonic chronicle which ends by perfectly duplicating the world and life.

The ceremony of the Labyrinth entwines its twists and turns with all those mirrors. The labyrinth is also duplication: a path that bifurcates into another, that bifurcates into another. Ah, that broad, endless garden with paths that bifurcate, each of whose branchings both imitates and differs from the previous ones, like men's actions or the meanings of words, a place where he who strolls or searches without a guide is lost forever! *Irremeabilis error*: an inextricable wandering, like reading, like dreams or memory. The very act of walking duplicates the wanderer, just as the sum of all the steps taken by a man finally makes a drawing, that of his own face. The poet's function is dual: on the one hand he fills the role of the monster in his labyrinth, self-segregated there; but he is also the killer of monsters who enters the labyrinth, coming from outside to finally recognize himself in the web of his turnings. Asterion prefers to die rather than abandon his complex home, which preserves him from a monstrousness that the eyes of others would proclaim; and Theseus realizes for one moment that he will never be able to get out of the labyrinth, that it contains no other key and no other horror than himself: "Expect nothing, not even / the beast in the black twilight." The labyrinth is a reiteration of duplications. That is why its prototype is the city or the library. Each patio in bustling Buenos Aires, the dreamed city, the mythic city, refers us to another patio, each street corner recalls another corner. We are yearners, inhabitants, and victims of the heavenly Jerusalem, whose streets we tread constantly even though the labyrinth that surrounds us may, according to circumstances, wish to call itself Buenos Aires, Paris, or

Vienna. But there is another place to get lost in that is even closer, the place of that forest of symbols, the library, which we traverse blindly, never finding the book that contains the key to all books or ever taking final possession of the *real* trees, tigers, and mountains promised by its pages. The library is the place of duplication par excellence. The word duplicates the thing but also duplicates the other occurrences of that same word or all words; Blake's tiger remits us to the tiger of the encyclopedia and that one to the tiger in travel books. The reader will never find either a genuine Ariadne's thread or the beast in this true labyrinth. There, the volumes hold in thrall civilizations, beliefs, and nations which, like Tlön and Uqbar, cannot be found outside, if this at least means anything. The mirror symbolizes the symbol; the labyrinth, our relationship with it.

The third instrument of duplication is the ceremony of the Imago Mundi. A summary of its ultimate meaning is given in Hermes Trismegistus' well-known formula: "What is above is equal to that which is below." Since the All is infinite, each part is also, in some sense, the All, and any one of the successive "alls" that we imagine is really nothing but a part. There are privileged spots where a very unusual concentration of perspectives exists, thanks to which a particular object acquires the virtue of irresistibly enlarging all its powers, thus repeating the universe. This is the case of the Aleph, which performs to perfection the purpose of the bad poet who has discovered it: to duplicate the world, not in the tedious extension of thousands of verses, but in one single spot and simultaneously, as a vertiginous vision capable of abolishing space and time. This irrefutable key to everything can be written on a leopard's skin, as the ascetic who is about to die between its claws discovers, or it can be the Zahir, that unforgettable object—coin, animal, landscape—which at last takes the place, in memory, of all other memories, making the person possessed by its image into an intensive Funes, no less of a usurper of the cosmos than the extensive one. The attempt to achieve the imago mundi is what, in the last instance, inspires the poet, who wants to find the word that dissolves—at the same instant abolishing them—all the marvels of the emperor's garden, so that the emperor will be obliged to decapitate him for having stolen his most precious possession. Did not Adam try, by eating the apple, to dispossess God from His beautiful garden? In Borges' latest book, *The Book of Sand*, there are two examples of imago mundi: one consists in the literature which tells of a certain lost people by means of a single word; the other is an infinite book which continually shows the images of all things in a flow impossible to grasp, so that the reader slips into an endless pursuit of them. Let us end with one last example, half jocular and half terrible, as so often happens with Borges: that of the wine cellar in Buenos Aires where the Trinity repeats its limitless glory before the innocent eyes of a little girl. The ceremony of the imago mundi alludes to an explosive, intuitive, nondiscursive duplication of the whole universe; if mirrors were symbols and labyrinths our commerce with them, the imago mundi is our yearning to possess the fullness of meaning without undergoing the effort and patience of mediation.

Faced with the All which splits into world and the discourse of the world, Borges is fascinated not by either of these two terms, but by the split itself. That split is precisely the literary function, the ambiguous secret of poets and philosophers. But duplication is a transition: no one can install himself in it with impunity. Borges pays for his stubborn installation in literary function with the aura of whimsical unreality that surrounds his work, an aura which has earned him the admiration of weak spirits who have made a poetic ensign out of superfluity and the hostility of those who abound so much in real problems that they never think of reality as a problem. It is an inevitable misunderstanding and probably an irrelevant one, for misunderstandings are the very fabric of reading. Need I insist, after writing these pages, that nothing is more alien to the disciplined and realistic Borges than whimsy or unreality? Yet it is useless to do so, for very few will believe me and he will never dispel the doubt. That is *his* secret.

# EPILOGUE

WHILE I WAS BUSY with the plan of this book and had already written the chapter entitled "The Storyteller Escapes," I read a lucid essay by Félix de Asúa on the novel, "El género neutro," in *Los Cuadernos de la Gaya Ciencia, II*, which has aroused me to new and disenchanted thoughts about the death of the story. The novel has turned out to be either the verbose autophagia of *Finnegans Wake* or the grunts and stammerings of Beckett's characters, lost in their corrupt limbo of impotence and desolation. "Light novels" are a parody or simulacrum, which betray the adventures they offer so freely through mere commercial convention or loss of nerve in the face of the sulfurous bubbling of the hero-less reality we are destined to inhabit. The novel has neutralized all genres in a sort of magma which we might call, with an expression drawn from the most recent linguistics, a "semantic marmalade." It has even assimilated and digested, after a fashion, that story or tale which I have tried to define in the first chapter of this book. *Treasure Island* and *The First Men in the Moon* are novels after all, no more and no less than *Absalom, Absalom!* or *Molloy*; moreover, they are novels that no one would dare to write nowadays except those second-class writers whose blessed bad taste anchors them in the past and lets them keep on telling stories out of it, as if time had not existed for them.

Ought we to speak of "narration-novels" versus "novel-novels"? In the former the tale, the story, is preserved like the insect imprisoned in a drop of amber, while the latter would be pure amber, in whose yellowish lividity no one could see his own face. Yet both cases are fatal from the viewpoint of that epic side of wisdom which is the story, according to Benjamin; since we see him only in his amber prison, the insect is a prehistoric specimen who can only be either dead or absent. The story is perpetuated in the translucent amalgam of the novel, which hides and deforms it no less than it reveals it; a solidified, stiff, inexplicable ancestor of itself, it seems more a corruption of the flawless purity that surrounds it than a prisoner or a relic. When the good taste and critical perspicacity of a period accept this and the bothersome guest has been dislodged, the amber's viscosity flows untrammeled, caring only for the repeated marvel of its empty self-reproduction. But what we never succeed in finding out about is the insect's free flight. For one thing is undeniable: the insect was born neither for the amber nor for annihilation but to fly in the open air. To express it somehow, what I am interested in is the insect, not the amber; the amber wearies me as much as those dishes that are excessively abundant and too much alike all through, a platter of spaghetti for instance, where you don't know which bores you sooner, the endless quantity or the monotonous sameness of its contents.

The question on this point is, Can the insect dissociate itself in any way from the amber? Because I will willingly turn over the amber to anyone capable of appreciating the hidden exquisiteness of its deceptive diversity or the perfectly planned magic of its construction. But what jungle do I have to go to if I want to find insects flying in joyous freedom? Have such creatures ever existed? May they not be a kind of shadow or secretion of the amber itself, which we innocents assume to be captive beings? Did they never really exist, perhaps? Did they exist once, but no more? Did their time pass away? Or, to abandon the metaphor of the trapped fly, which is getting a little irksome, I ask myself if it will not be possible to free the story from the novel's fossilizing, sticky grip; in short, if it is possible to rescue the story from literature and return it to its real terrain: morality, initiation, or magic.

I will not pretend to give an answer that I do not know. I will not cry enthusiastically that the tale cannot die while men live because everything can die as long as men last, beginning with men themselves. I find all other disappearances both minor and plausible. But neither are there definitive reasons that oblige us to admit that the death of the novel or even the death of all literature must presuppose the abolition of all stories. There are even fairly weighty indications that support the opposite view. The most evident of these is one whose very obviousness disconcerts and perturbs us: literature has history, but the story does not. History has become the most important thing we possess in order to think about any of the realities which surround us, to such a point that to say of something that it lacks history or historicity—so as not to confuse this use of the word *history* with the other which we have given it as the equivalent of *tale* or *story*—seems like a very grave sin of the worst sort of idealizing Platonism. And yet I feel that it is perfectly evident that the conventional metamorphoses undergone by the story— in the sense of the word that we established in the first chapter— neither justify nor allow a historical analysis of it, while such an analysis is perfectly appropriate in the case of the novel or the theater as literary forms. To return to a previous metaphor, the amber is historical but the insect is not; and in the cases where the insect is also historical, he is so in his aspect as a prisoner of the amber. Historians find infinite fodder for commentary in the mythic imagination or the stylistic resources of the *Odyssey* compared with the very different ones of *Treasure Island*, for example; but I maintain that, insofar as both are tales or narrations, there is no temporal difference between them or historical precedence or a classifiable flow of information that explains the transition from Ulysses to Jim Hawkins.

All stories are coetaneous, all occupy the same plane in time; that is, *outside* time. The old Chinese ghost story—which comes to us from before the Christian era—is neither prior in time nor antecedent in form with respect to any story by Montague Rhodes James; both are the fruit of a strictly identical spirit, at least insofar as the gradual differences recorded by the historian are concerned. On the other hand, from Flaubert to Proust and from Proust to Philippe Sollers or Juan Benet, a line is spun that is fundamentally composed of time, of the accumulation of innovations and disillusionments. That is history. Literature is its offspring, but pure storytelling is of a different lineage, in which everything returns, nothing is forgotten, and the same action is preserved and repeated, intact, only to be brought to new birth. To express it in another way, in the story many things happen, but nothing happens to the story; in the novel, though, almost nothing ever happens, but things keep happening to the novel, about which the specialized reviews are likely to give us immediate information. What the novel recounts— what is recounted *in* the novel—consists of the adventures of the novel itself; what I have called pure storytelling, on the other hand, at once refers us to the possibility of action, to the world of what is still left to be done rather than the area of what is still left to tell, even though the second of these may return immediately and joyously after the first. Owing to this different situation with regard to time, the novel necessarily ends in death, while the story narrates the conquest of the fullness of life. And this being true, since it is outside history, no matter how heretical this statement may seem, how could storytelling die? Is not that precisely the only possibility which is closed to it? That the novel should eventually die is a normal thing, inscribed on its very nature. The story, however, ensconced in the limbo of nonhistory, seems alien to death no less than to time itself. Obviously this can be a mistaken impression. As I have already said, perhaps the insect is no more than a chance configuration of the amber, and the inevitable destiny of the amber will also destroy the insect. But what gives me hope is the annoyance or scorn of good novelists, of serious students of literature, in the face of the storytellers' ingenuous insistence on continuing to tell their stories no matter what, without worrying one whit about the evolution of novelistic resources during the last half century. "It seems that time doesn't pass for them!" they say with astonished indignation. And indeed, no: it does not pass. Maybe the secret of their immortality resides in that.

But there is another argument in favor of the perennial nature of stories, a testimony so subjective that I have not dared to speak of it until the last pages of this impudently subjective book. The moment for confession has arrived. There are spirits—I know only my own case, but modesty prevents me

from considering myself inconceivably unique—who understand everything in the form of a story and are hopelessly closed
to any art or knowledge that cannot be told. I hasten to recognize the fact that this is a tremendous limitation. I cannot
hear a symphony without simultaneously inventing a plot about
fountains and storms; behind every Beethoven quartet I discern
a passionate love story, and I prefer the opera to any other type
of music because it obviously tells something. Each painting
and each piece of sculpture are fragments of a story that I hasten
to reconstruct in my mind in order to enjoy them, architecture
interests me solely as the decor for adventures which I immediately sense written on the strange solitude of the stones. Forests, or the sea, do not attract me except in the measure that
they are the ancient setting for the epic—unsung by any
Homer—of the animals, who were our gods and in some sense
will be our gods again. Religion is the best story of all, the plot
that underlies all stories; its dogmatic perplexities or casuistical
theology strike me as only the mistakes of bad storytellers,
incapable of awakening their hearers' interest because of their
mania for getting entangled in digressions. I am self-confessedly
blind to the formal magic of mathematics or logic; on the other
hand, I greatly enjoy the nooks and corners of history, philosophy, and politics. Science and love interest me because of their
relationship with ethics, which endows each action with the
weight of legend. Any affair in which one cannot be the hero
of one's own passion is absolutely alien and superfluous for me.
In poetry, I like the epic that is apt to reside within all lyric
poetry, but the impassioned accumulation of metaphors which
repel any articulation of plot, or the avant-garde spirit which
brings together with no visible thread of connection penguins
and neon lights or despair and umbrellas, bores me beyond
description. In literature, I need hardly say, I am annoyed by
all verbal experimentation, except in especially fortunate cases
like Joyce or Faulkner, when I am convinced that the story
could not be told better by any other means. I know that this
is a limitation, and I do not glory in it; but we must use to our
advantage the shortcomings that afflict us. My enjoyment of
storytelling allows me, for instance, to have a very pleasant

relationship with imbeciles. When I have to deal with someone whose ideas I detest or whose opinions merit only scorn I try to lead him to the terrain of storytelling and make him tell me something; even the meanest creatures harbor a painful or dreadful odyssey. Persons whom I would not be able to endure in any other way manage to amuse me and—who knows?— even interest me as storytellers. Conversely, I have no lack of friends whom I adore but whose presence soon becomes unbearable to me because they have no gift for telling anything and have a mania for sticking to the abstract or the doctrinaire. One would like to say to the unwelcome guest, "Tell your story and get out!" But this procedure, should it become general, would perhaps simplify human relationships to an undesirable degree.

Is it absurd to suppose that as long as there are people affected by the curse of an insatiable desire for stories, incapable of considering wisdom or love outside the prism of the narrative, useless for any other viewpoint on action except the hero's viewpoint—is it absurd to suppose that as long as there are incurable invalids of myths, like me, stories will endure even though all the literature and all the culture we now know disappear? But if time is as strong as it seems to be, if nothing can escape the erosion of history, and if, dragged down into the maelstrom of the years, stories finally disappear from man's word and man's memory, I solemnly promise to come back to life and tell you some.

# ENVOI

The night is full of taverns and castles, and in each of them are animal skins, weapons, roaring chimney-fires, men mighty as trees, and never a clock.

Ernest Bloch, *Das Prinzip Hoffnung*

# BIOBIBLIOGRAPHICAL GUIDE
# TO THE CHIEF
# AUTHORS MENTIONED

ANDERSON, KENNETH. [b. 1910] Big-game hunter and writer. I do not have his biographical data at hand, though I suppose that the apogee of his Indian adventures must have been in the second and third decades of this century. As principal works we may mention *Man-eaters* and *Jungle Killers, The Tiger Roars,* and *The Black Panther of Sivanipalli.*

BORGES, JORGE LUIS. Born in Buenos Aires in 1899. He is, indisputably, one of the really great poets and storytellers this century has produced. Universal recognition of his work has been late but overwhelming. The devotee of Borges—he is a whole type of literature in himself—does not make choices among Borges' books: he chooses Borges, and that is enough. Still, we will mention some titles: *Fictions, The Aleph, Labyrinths, Other Inquisitions, Dreamtigers, The Book of Sand* . . . and all his poetry.

CARR, JOHN DICKSON. Has also signed his novels with the pseudonym Carter Dickson. Born in Pennsylvania in 1905. He lives in London, where he is secretary of the Detection Club. In my opinion he is one of the three or four "greats" of the detective-story genre. He is distinguished by a certain taste for introducing a fantastic or impossible element in setting forth his cases, in which the why is frequently more important than the who. In one of his best novels, *The Burning Court,* two solutions are offered for a crime, the first strictly rationalistic and the second supernatural. He has invented a protagonist, Dr. Gideon Fell, whose physical appearance was directly modeled on Chesterton's. Some of his novels are: *The Black Spectacles; The Eight of Swords; Fire, Burn!; The Waxworks Murder; The Red Widow Murders; The Unicorn Murders.* He is also the author of a pleasant biography of Sir Arthur Conan Doyle.

CHRISTIE, AGATHA. English novelist, born 1891, died 1976. It is not difficult—indeed, it is inevitable—to find fault with this classic writer of the detective story, whose very prolific work spreads over more than half a century of uninterrupted publication. But it would be fairer to recognize her tireless ingenuity, the subtlety of plots that are much less obvious than they appear at first sight, the charm of anachronistically Victorian characters and situations in which an element of gentle irony is never lacking. Gratitude for the delightful hours her calculated puzzles have given us is stronger, in this instance, than critical zeal. Let us recall some of her masterworks: *The ABC Murders, The Murder of Roger Ackroyd, Lord Edgware Dies, Ten Little Indians, Three Blind Mice, The Labors of Hercules.*

CROMPTON, RICHMAL. I believe Crompton was a schoolmistress or something along those lines, and I know that she died in the late 1960s, at about eighty years of age. For me, her existence is no less problematical than that of the Castaneda who invented, or listened to, Don Juan. Is Don Juan another aspect of Castaneda? Was Richmal Crompton—pepper-and-salt wig, old-fashioned black dress, lorgnette fastened with a broad ribbon—William's most successful disguise? It would not be the first time he disguised himself as a grandmother, the better to carry his plans to a successful conclusion.

DOYLE, SIR ARTHUR CONAN. Novelist, born in Scotland in 1859, died in 1930. One of the purest and most fabulous storytellers in the English language. Sherlock Holmes is a monument sufficient to make any writer immortal. Doyle also created Professor Challenger, the honorable and hard-fighting Sir Nigel Loring, and his endearingly swashbuckling Brigadier Gerard. He is distinguished by an enviable facility for what is interesting, a disposition toward the macabre and fantastic which do honor to his northern blood, and a perfect command of how to narrate action. He dreamed of being another Walter Scott; he actually was something else but by no means inferior.

GREY, ZANE. Born in Zanesville, Ohio, in 1875, died in Altadena, California, in 1939. He was a dentist in New York from 1898 to 1904. He published his first book, *Betty Garey*, in 1902. Founding father of the Western novel, he has had imitators but in general his works have never been improved upon. Among his hundreds of books worth mentioning are *The Spirit of the Border* and *Riders of the Purple Sage*.

LONDON, JACK. Born in San Francisco in 1876, he died in 1916. He was the son of a traveling astrologer (whom he never knew) and a mother who was an adept of spiritualism. After a poverty-stricken childhood, during which he went to work in a factory at thirteen, he was a seal hunter in Japan, a highway laborer in Canada and the United States, and a gold-seeker in Alaska. By sheer force of will he taught himself until he achieved a broad culture. He was passionately attached to the progressivist ideas of his era, joining the American Socialist party. He succeeded in gaining a reputation as a journalist and novelist, becoming one of the most popular writers of his time.

His first novels, set in the Great North, earned him the sobriquet of "Kipling of the snows." His extraordinary narrative gifts, ambiguously illuminated by a touching need to aspire to a fraternal kind of society, found expression in his passion for wild, lonely places and adventure and in his ferociously pessimistic view of man. He was fascinated by the terrible, the violent, and the supernatural; he dreamed of cycles of evolution and the future course of history. He became very rich, squandered his fortune, traveled incessantly, had two stormy marriages. Haunted by the ghosts of alcohol and the specter of fate, he committed suicide on his California ranch, Glen Ellen, in 1916. Within his admirable body of work I would like to mention here his rude sagas *The Call of the Wild* and *White Fang*, his autobiographical *Martin Eden*, his splendid *The Sea Wolf*, and his alarming visions of an extremely remote past, *Before Adam*, and a desolate future, *The Iron Heel*.

LOVECRAFT, H[OWARD] P[HILLIPS]. Born in Providence, R.I., in 1890, he died in the same city in 1937. He led a twilight existence of solitude and poverty, with no other encouragement than an incessant correspondence with a relatively small circle of youthful admirers. His astonishing tales of terror aroused little interest during his lifetime but today have become an obsession unlike any other. Their central theme is a whole peculiar cosmology and mythology, based on the experience of man's desperate helplessness when confronted with the fathomless forces that have produced him and will destroy him. Anyone who really gets into one of his stories cannot bear not to read all the rest.

MAY, KARL. Karl Hohenthal (his real name) was born in Saxony in 1842 and died in Radebeul in 1912. In an effort to overcome the poverty of his humble origins, he traveled while still very young through Europe, North and South America, Kurdistan, Arabia, the Pacific islands, etc., having adventures which apparently placed him on the side of the outlaws rather than that of the "good guys" of his stories. His books attained enormous popularity in Germany and have been widely translated. The saga of Old Shatterhand and Winnetou, his most successful literary creation, includes the novels *La montaña de oro* [The Mountain of Gold], *La venzanza de Winnetou* [The Vengeance of Winnetou], *En la boca del lobo* [In the Wolf's Mouth], and *La isla del desierto* [The Desert Island].

POE, EDGAR ALLAN. American poet and storyteller of genius, born in Baltimore, Md., in 1813, died in the same city on Sunday, October 7, 1849. His life was ruined by poverty; a keen intelligence and alcohol combined to produce a wonderful body of literary work, darkly sumptuous, extremely refined, humorous, an authentic miracle of fantastic romanticism. All his stories, his poems, even his critical essays, are indispensable. Whoever has not read "The Black Cat," "The Pit and the Pendulum," *The Facts in the Case of M. Valdemar, The Adventures of Arthur Gordon Pym,* or "The Gold Bug," still does not know to what point reading can be both a dangerous and a joyous operation. His complete works have had the good fortune to be translated into Spanish by Julio Cortázar (their fate in French was even luckier, for they were translated by Baudelaire).

SALGARI, EMILIO. Born in Verona in 1863. In his youth he was a sailor, traveling all over the world. Then he took up journalism and storytelling. He wrote 86 novels and more than 100 short stories, in which he recreates the many faces of adventure, the dangers of jungle and ocean, the restless turns and twists of pure action which seeks only to perpetuate itself. Poverty and family misfortunes drove him to suicide in Turin in 1911. He deserves inclusion in the history of literature for his titles alone: *La montaña de luz* [The Mountain of Light], *El león de Damasco* [The Lion of Damascus], *El capitán Tormenta* [Captain Storm], *El rey de los cangrejos* [The King of the Crabs], *La galera del bajá* [The Pasha's Galley], *El desierto de fuego* [The Fiery

Desert], *Los solitarios del océano* [Alone on the Ocean], *Los tigres de la Malasia* [The Tigers of Malaysia], etc.

STEVENSON, ROBERT LOUIS. The king of contemporary storytellers was born in Edinburgh in 1850. After a Bohemian youth, during which he desultorily studied law, he turned his full attention to literature. No one has understood the necessary ambiguity of the story as well as he, an ambiguity which is not contradicted but is reinforced with an implacable moral passion. Possessor of an infallible taste for good plots, he is able to develop them in a splendid and effective style which never sacrifices the poetic element; his way of telling stories is not superimposed on them but seems to grow naturally with them. Besides *Treasure Island*, a sober saga of audacity and moral problems which is one of the few perfect achievements of modern literature, he endowed our imaginations with the archetype of the man whose moral split is realized in physical form: *The Strange Case of Dr. Jekyll and Mr. Hyde*. His *New Arabian Nights* carries the detective story to dreamlike dimensions without diminishing its capricious conventions. The myth of Cain and Abel was cast in unforgettable form in *The Master of Ballantrae*, while *David Balfour, Catriona,* and *In the South Seas* have become classics of their respective genres. His unfinished *The Weir of Hermiston* poses for the last time in his work the evil and necessary mystery of obedience and power. Affected by a serious pulmonary illness, he spent the last years of his life traveling from island to island in the South Seas, perhaps seeking the mystic land of perfect health. The Samoans called him Tusitala, "the teller of tales." He died on Upolu in 1894 and was buried by the natives on Mt. Vaea, as he had wished. The epitaph in verse which he himself composed begins:

> Under the wide and starry sky
> Dig the grave and let me lie:
> Glad did I live and gladly die. . . .

TOLKIEN, J[OHN] R[ONALD] R[EUEL]. Born in 1892 and died in 1974. He was professor of Old English literature at Oxford, publishing studies on and versions of the Old English poems *Sir Gawain and the Green Knight, Pearl,* and *Sir Orfeo*. In 1938 he began to write *The Lord of the Rings*, which was to be published sixteen years later; the previous year (1937) *The Hobbit* had been published, a short novel in which Tolkien first took possession of Middle-earth. We, his devotees, who do not want to be expelled from that dubious paradise, are awaiting anxiously the publication of his posthumous novel *The Silmarillion* [New York: Houghton Mifflin, 1977].

VERNE, JULES. Born in Nantes in 1828, he died in Amiens in 1905. He completed law studies and worked as a stockbroker until finally turning exclusively to literature. The enthusiasm aroused by his work brought him fame and wealth. Much more interesting than his celebrated faculty for anticipating the future triumphs of science is his unerring instinct for discovering the mythical archetypes that those triumphs would create. Perhaps no one has dreamed of *spaces* and *instruments* with such happy precision. In addition to the two works dealt with in this book, let us mention *Five Weeks in a Balloon, The Children of Captain Grant, Two Years of Vacation, Hector Servadac, The Mysterious Island, Dick Sands: A Captain at Fifteen, From the Earth to the Moon,* and *Michael Strogoff.*

WELLS, H[ERBERT] G[EORGE]. Novelist, journalist, and popularizer of scientific, historical, and political subjects. He was born in Kent in 1866 and died in London in 1946. His regenerationist obsession— "human history becomes more and more a race between education and catastrophe"—reduced neither the energy nor the imagination of his social and political parables, which are appreciated today for quite other reasons than their author's good intentions. In addition to the two books discussed here, let us mention *The Island of Dr. Moreau, The Invisible Man, The Time Machine, When the Sleeper Wakes, Twelve Stories and a Dream,* and *Kipps.*

And a last, final salute to all those authors mentioned in passing who could have taken up many pages, to the authors I have forgotten, to those I have unjustly left out for reasons unknown both to reason and the heart, to those who have slipped out of the book heaven knows why:

RUDYARD KIPLING, incomparable creator of Mowgli and Kim; SIR [HENRY] RIDER HAGGARD, who told me the tremendous adventure of Allan Quatermain in King Solomon's mines, and how the beauty of the ages-old sorceress dissolved in the flaming Fountain of Life; EDGAR RICE BURROUGHS, to whom I owe the great, agile figure of Tarzan and so many astounding adventures on Mars and Venus; JAMES OLIVER CURWOOD, whose animal biographies—*Kazan, Bari, The Grizzly King*—I find stupendous, even comparable to London's *White*

*Fang*; JAMES FENIMORE COOPER and his romantic Mohicans; SIR WAL-
TER SCOTT, the Wizard of the North, whose *Ivanhoe* and *The Talisman*
it is unpardonable not to have mentioned; the musketeerly eloquence
of ALEXANDRE DUMAS; GASTON LEROUX, whose lovelorn Rouleta-
bille—whoever had a name like that!—discovered that the impossible
murderer of the Yellow Room was his own father, just as Freud could
have told him if he had been consulted; the unforgettable noble bandits, like Dick Turpin battling the thousand police chiefs who pursued
him, or the refined Arsène Lupin bestowed on us by MAURICE LE-
BLANC; the legendary travels of MARCO POLO, so minute in his descriptions of the exotically different, whose Venetian world is now almost
as disconcertingly exotic as the world of Kublai Khan that he described
for us; the too-serious writers exiled to the kindergarten by an adult
world that failed to listen to their metaphysics (HERMAN MELVILLE),
their satire (JONATHAN SWIFT), or their wildly extravagant humor
(LEWIS CARROLL); RAFAEL SABATINI's foils and masks, JEAN RAY and
his crowd of fantastic Flemings; the terrible, sleepless children of
MARK TWAIN, perhaps the most ferocious pessimist of modern literature; CAPTAIN MARRYAT's youthful adventurers; ROBERT E. HOW-
ARD, inventor of the Conan saga, who committed suicide at the age
of twenty-nine because he could not bear to see his mother die, and
all his brothers of sword and sorcery: FRITZ LEIBER, MICHAEL MOOR-
COCK, and so on; the bewitched rightists of DENNIS WHEATLEY;
MAYNE REID's plant hunters and slow caravans; the "greats" of science
fiction, like RAY BRADBURY, with his homesick explorers marooned
on Mars, or ISAAC ASIMOV; ARTHUR C. CLARKE, philosopher and
poet of technology's inexhaustible promises, which will make man
something more or less than a man; and last but not least, the true
and pure storytellers, CHARLES PERRAULT, the Brothers GRIMM, HANS
CHRISTIAN ANDERSEN, and the anonymous taletellers who dreamed
of Sinbad and Aladdin during the thousand and one nights of childhood perpetually lost and regained.

# NOTES

## 1. THE STORYTELLER ESCAPES

1. *Gilgamesh*, version by William Ellery Leonard (New York: Viking Press, 1934), p. 5.

2. After finishing this chapter, I find this remark in Schopenhauer which, within its obvious differences, I believe fundamentally refers to the distinction I established between primary and secondary conventions, though Schopenhauer considers only the latter to be properly speaking conventional: "The distinction, so often discussed in our day, between *classic* and *romantic* poetry seems to me to rest ultimately on the fact that the former knows none but purely human, actual, and natural motives; the latter, on the other hand, maintains as effective also motives that are pretended, conventional, and imaginary. Among such motives are those springing from the Christian myth, then those of the chivalrous, exaggerated, and fantastic principle of honour, and further those of the absurd and ridiculous Christian-Germanic veneration of women, and finally those of doting and moonstruck hyperphysical amorousness." (*The World as Will and Representation*, trans. E. F. J. Payne. Indian Hills, Colo.: The Falcon's Wing Press, 1958, vol. 2, ch. 37.)

3. Michael Innes, *Hamlet, Revenge!* (London: Victor Gollancz, 1937), p. 45.

4. Walter Benjamin, "The Storyteller," in *Illuminations*, trans. Harry Zohn (New York: Harcourt, Brace & World, 1968). All quotations in this chapter, except where otherwise indicated, come from this essay.

5. Jorge Luis Borges, "Prólogo," in *La invención de Morel* (Madrid-Buenos Aires: Alianza-Emecé, 1972), pp. 9–10.

6. Goethe, J. W. von, *Poetry and Truth*, trans. Minna Steele Smith (London: G. Bell and Sons, 1913), vol. 1, p. 29.

7. An entirely new viewpoint is adopted by Dieter Wellershoff when he says, "It is true that the white spot behind the story was covered for a while by apparent evolutionary processes. Now everybody is there again, in the empty duration of 'it's not worth the trouble to go on telling.' The white spot behind the story is the known that is unknown, everyday life. Its faceless horror leaps out at one from the laconic formula at the end of tales: 'and if

they're not dead, they live there still.' Consequently, that is all that can still be said about them. One lives, but it would be exactly the same if one were dead. After people have found their place in life, after cavilations, errors, and dangers, life takes the form of a repetition unbroken by novelty. One normal working day is just like another, and since there is nothing new to hope for, the past is placed above the present and the future as their inevitable, always familiar model. In this way the 'happy ending' can be understood as pointing toward depression. Like a broken record, we hear the speaker's voice going on talking. But saying, always and exclusively, 'and so on, and so on, and so on.'" (*Literatur und Lustprinzip.* Cologne: Kiepenheuer & Witsch, 1973, p. 77.)

Here Wellershoff ignores two fundamental characteristics of the story. On the one hand, empty everydayness is the terrain of the person who has nothing to tell, the author who has never been anywhere, while a story tells precisely the unexpected event which confers on everydayness its character of being won, its consistency as a prize, its joyous resting on what has been conquered and the shared memory of adventure. Storytelling recounts the chance journey offered to the person who, by following that path, dares an intense every-dayness; even nostalgia contributes to this. On the other hand, the end of a story is always provisional; the story ends, but stories do not. The story can continue at any moment and, after "if they're not dead, they live there still," which marks a pause, also certifying the story's vitality, can pulse as many other stories as the one that has been told. In any case, Wellershoff's comment has a broad field of suitable application to different kinds of "happy endings"; to the edifying "committed" stories about political awareness, to those of cures by ordinary psychoanalysts, to those of American comedies, and the infrequent and terribly ironic ones in some Bergman films.

8. José Bergamín, *Fronteras infernales de la poesía* (Madrid: Taurus, 1959), p. 20.

9. Borges, "Prólogo," p. 10.

## 2. A TREASURE OF AMBIGUITY

1. If we do not count Captain Flint, whose ghost haunts the whole tale, and the parrot of the same name who serves as his ironic spokesman.

## 3. THE JOURNEY DOWNWARD

1. I give herewith a more detailed description of the initiatory adventure, whose conciseness, in my opinion, makes it particularly complete. "The mythological hero, setting forth from his commonday hut or castle, is lured, carried away, or else voluntarily proceeds, to the threshold of adventure. There he encounters a shadow presence that guards the passage. The hero may defeat or conciliate this power and go alive into the kingdom of the dark

(brother-battle, dragon-battle; offering, charm), or be slain by the opponent and descend in death (dismemberment, crucifixion). Beyond the threshold, then, the hero journeys through a world of unfamiliar yet strangely intimate forces, some of which severely threaten him (tests), some of which give magical aid (helpers). When he arrives at the nadir of the mythological round, he undergoes a supreme ordeal and gains his reward. The triumph may be represented as the hero's sexual union with the goddess-mother of the world (sacred marriage), his recognition by the father-creator (father atonement), his own divinization (apotheosis), or again—if the powers have remained unfriendly to him—his theft of the boon he came to gain (bride-theft, fire-theft); intrinsically it is an expansion of consciousness and therewith of being (illumination, transfiguration, freedom). The final work is that of the return. If the powers have blessed the hero, he now sets forth under their protection (emissary); if not, he flees and is pursued (transformational flight, obstacle flight). At the return threshold the transcendental powers must remain behind; the hero re-emerges from the kingdom of dread (return, resurrection). The boon that he brings restores the world (elixir)." (Joseph Campbell, *The Hero with a Thousand Faces*. Princeton: Princeton University Press, 1968, pp. 245–46.)

2. See Simone Vierne, *Jules Verne et le roman initiatique* (Paris: Ed. du Sirac, 1973).

## 10. AMONG THE FAIRIES

1. Paul Kocher, *Master of Middle-earth* (London: Thames and Hudson, 1972).

2. Randel Helms, *Tolkien's World* (London: Thames and Hudson, 1974).

3. See, for example, C. S. Lewis' book *That Hideous Strength* (1945; reprint ed., London: Pan Books, 1974). We find the struggle between a company of noble characters, led by Merlin the magician, and the evil forces of diabolical scientism. Ideologically and religiously the story is much more specific than Tolkien's, but it is infinitely inferior in narrative interest.

## 13. THE MURDERER WHO LEAVES NO CLUES

1. Michael Innes, *Hamlet, Revenge!* (New York: Penguin, 1976); Innes, *There Came Both Mist and Snow* (London: Victor Gollancz, 1940). [U.S. title *A Comedy of Terrors* (New York: Dodd, Mead, 1940)].

2. An excellent article by Félix de Asúa, "El género neutro," in *Los Cuadernos de la Gaya Ciencia, II* (Madrid, October 1975), to which I refer again in the epilogue of this book, supports these views.

3. G. K. Chesterton, Dorothy L. Sayers, John Dickson Carr, and others collaborated on this curious novel, whose interest is fundamentally extra-literary. Each wrote a chapter and, independently of the others, proposed a

solution. [Detection Club, *The Floating Admiral* (Boston, Mass.: Gregg Press, 1979)]

4. *Informaciones*, Madrid, 1976.

5. Few cases of literary vitality are as impressive as Sherlock Holmes'. Since the death of his creator Conan Doyle—if we can speak so improperly, for it would be more exact to say "his vehicle" or something of the sort—he continues a career that shows no signs of ending. Sir Arthur's son, Adrian Conan Doyle, wrote a series of new Holmes cases. Ellery Queen placed him in confrontation with Jack the Ripper in an excellent novel that was later made into a film. H. F. Heard won all our affection in his *A Taste for Honey*, a surprising problem solved by a hundred-year-old Sherlock working incognito. Very recently two fine novels have again placed the great detective of Baker Street in the forefront of current literature. The first of these, Nicholas Meyer's *The Seven-Per-Cent Solution*, brings Holmes together with another great Victorian investigator, young Sigmund Freud, and has them work together in a desperate attempt to save the political equilibrium of Europe. The second is *The Return of Moriarty*, by John Gardner; the book's protagonist is Holmes' archenemy, while the detective himself does not even appear. The novel is a matchless chronicle of London low-life at the end of the nineteenth century, but it also contains an interesting disquisition on what it means to be guilty and what it means to be loyal.

6. François de Lyonnais, "Idées," in *La Littérature potentielle*, ed. Oulipo (Paris: Gallimard, 1973), p. 66.

7. I am not satisfied with the sour tone of my reference to Mrs. Christie. Maybe what I have said in it is fair, but it gives the impression of a hostility I am far from feeling for the woman who has been one of my favorite female authors, the sincere and Platonic love of my adolescence. I express this feeling of uneasiness after finishing the reading of Poirot's last case, that *Curtain* which closes his career. The story is an admirable recapitulation of all its writer's themes, a masterly and reflective view of all the genre's ambiguities. Poirot and Hastings return to Styles, scene of their first case, to begin a twilit adventure in a cleverly evoked, deadly atmosphere of advancing age and decline. They confront a strange kind of murderer, whom we might call a "catalytic criminal," a sort of precipitator of the murderous longings we all harbor within us and which can lead us to crime in order to erase what we find intolerable in our lives. This murderer does not brandish the pistol or administer the poison: he confines himself to *being present* in an atmosphere appropriate for homicide, and to murmuring as if by mistake the words that will unleash the indecisive criminal's fury. All the characters in *Curtain* feel his deadly influence, even good old Hastings, who briefly recovers that ominous first-person whisper behind which Roger Ackroyd's murderer was concealed. In the end it is Poirot who kills, with Hastings' innocent cooperation, and not less than twice! In some sense, has it not always been this way? Is not Poirot himself that presence which attracts crime, in a way, which

seeks it and enjoys it, like the criminal he pursues at Styles? But also, is this not the inevitable role of the reader himself who is a detective-story fan? This last case does away in one stroke with the criminal, the detective, and the voyeur who harasses them with his unsleeping eye. The infinite ambiguity of the "justice" meted out in these stories is made perfectly clear in Poirot's last words: "By taking ——'s life, I have saved other lives—innocent lives. But still I do not know. . . . It is perhaps right that I should not know. I have always been so sure—too sure. . . ." Thus ends the career of a detective for whom, to seek his equal, we would have to go all the way back to Sherlock Holmes. As a final lesson, we learn that the crime is indissolubly linked to the *plan* of liberation through which, out of our mutilated lives, we dream of happiness; in a sense all of us would be ready to kill in order to become immortal. Perhaps the real murderer is not the perpetrator of the deed but the observer who sniffs it out as if it were a question of a hunting trophy, or the avid spectator who desires it. And yet the resplendent joy of the hero appears for a moment in Poirot's farewell, dedicated to those of us who have admired him for so many years: "Yes, they have been good days . . . !" A beautiful farewell, Agatha, old girl! My brilliant, my subtle, my disconcerting Agatha Christie! My hat is off to you!

# NOTE ON ILLUSTRATIONS

Chapter 2: "The Map of Treasure Island," drafted by Robert Louis Stevenson before he began writing *Treasure Island*. Chapter 3: From an early edition of *Twenty Thousand Leagues Under the Sea,* by Jules Verne. Chapter 4: Illustration by Thomas Henry for the first edition of *William's Crowded Hours,* by Richmal Crompton. Chapter 5: Reprinted from *Il corsaro Nero,* by Emilio Salgari (Edizione integrale annotato. Milan: © 1970 Arnoldo Mondadore Editore), p. 198. Chapter 6: Illustration by Gamba for the first edition of *La Regina dei Caraibi,* by Emilio Salgari. Chapter 7: "War of the Worlds" cover illustration by Frank R. Paul, *Amazing Stories* (August 1927), Vol. 2, No. 4. Chapter 8: Jacket design by Barbara Swiderska for the English-language edition of William Bazé's *Tiger! Tiger!* (New York: Abelard-Schuman, 1966; text © 1957 Elek Books Ltd.). Chapter 9: Illustration by Leonard Everett Fisher for *The Star Rover,* by Jack London (New York: © 1963 The Macmillan Company). Chapter 10: Illustration by J. R. R. Tolkien for *The Hobbit,* 3d ed. (Boston: Houghton Mifflin; London: George Allen & Unwin, 1966; © 1966 J. R. R. Tolkien). Chapter 11: Jacket illustration by Woodruff for a reprint edition of Zane Grey's *Wanderer of the Wasteland.* Chapter 12: Illustration by Ferat for "The Pit and the Pendulum," from *Complete Works of Edgar Allan Poe,* vol. 5, James A. Harrison, ed. (New York: Fred de Fau, 1902). Chapter 13: Illustration by Sidney Paget for *The Hound of the Baskervilles,* chapter xii, "Death on the

Moor," in *The Strand Magazine* (London), February 1902, vol. 23.    Chapter 14: "The Cretan Labyrinth: With the Story of Theseus and Ariadne"; Florentine, about 1460–70; in Arthur M. Hind, *Early Italian Engraving,* vol. 2, plate 101 (London; Knoedler, 1938).